THE COST OF DOING BUSINESS

STUDY, 2019 EDITION

NAHB®
National Association
of Home Builders

The Cost of Doing Business Study, 2019 Edition

BuilderBooks, a Service of the National Association of Home Builders

Patricia Potts	Senior Director
Calli Schmidt	Editor
Joe Rudden	Cover Design
Robert Brown	Composition

Gerald M. Howard	Chief Executive Officer
Robert Dietz	Senior Vice President and Chief Economist, Economics and Housing Policy
Paul Emrath	Vice President, Economics and Housing Policy
Rose Quint	Assistant Vice President, Survey Research, Economics and Housing Policy
Marcia Childs	Director, Business Management Department

Disclaimer

This publication provides accurate information on the subject matter covered. The publisher is selling it with the understanding that the publisher is not providing legal, accounting, or other professional service. If you need legal advice or other expert assistance, obtain the services of a qualified professional experienced in the subject matter involved. The NAHB has used commercially reasonable efforts to ensure that the contents of this volume are complete and appear without error; however the NAHB makes no representations or warranties regarding the accuracy and completeness of this document's contents. The NAHB specifically disclaims any implied warranties of merchantability or fitness for a particular purpose. The NAHB shall not be liable for any loss of profit or any other commercial damages, including but not limited to incidental, special, consequential or other damages. Reference herein to any specific commercial products, process, or service by trade name, trademark, manufacturer, or otherwise does not necessarily constitute or imply its endorsement, recommendation, or favored status by the NAHB. The views and opinions of the author expressed in this publication do not necessarily state or reflect those of the NAHB, and they shall not be used to advertise or endorse a product.

Published in the United States of America

23 22 21 20   2 3 4 5

ISBN-13: 978-0-86718-770-0
eISBN-13: 978-0-86718-771-7

For further information, please contact:
National Association of Home Builders
1201 15th Street, NW
Washington, DC 20005-2800
BuilderBooks.com

Contents

Figures

Tables

Chapter 6. Production Builders

Chapter 9. Historical Data And Trends

Acknowledgments

The NAHB Economics and Housing Policy Group conducted the survey and tabulated the findings. The NAHB Business Management and Information Technology Committee provided oversight because it has jurisdiction over matters relating to improving the business management skills of NAHB builder members to enhance their competitiveness, profitability, and professionalism.

In accordance with NAHB strategic plan objectives, the committee makes policy recommendations on business management issues, develops educational programs, writes and publishes manuals, conducts business management research, and provides consulting assistance to other committees.

The committee's mission statement is
"To serve as the leading resource to the building industry in the areas of management, finance, information technology, operations, and human resources"

Members of the 2018 Business Management & Information Technology Committee

Brandon Bryant, CGP, Master CGP, Red Tree Builders

Vince Butler, CAPS, CGR, GMB, GMR, Butler Brothers Corp.

Don Colegrove, University of Louisiana-Monroe

Robert Criner, CAPS, CGB, CGP, CGR, GMB, GMR, Criner Remodeling

Teri Edwards, Carteret County HBA

John Gunkelman, CAPS, CGB, CGP, CGR, Dakota Construction of Fargo Inc.

Darrick Guthmiller, CAPS, CGB, Kochmann Brothers Homes Inc.

Alan Hanbury Jr., CAPS, CGP, CGR, GMR, House of Hanbury Builders Inc.

Alicia Huey, AGH Homes Inc.

Mark Hutchings, Brigham Young University

RL Johnson, CAPS, Right at Home Technologies

John Jones, SoftPlan Systems Inc.

Joel Katz, CGP, GMB, Katz Builders Inc.

Gary Kerns, Gary Kerns Homebuilders LLC

Mark Konter, Konter Quality Homes Inc.

Mitch Levinson, CAPS, CGP, CMP, CSP, MIRM, Marketing RELEVANCE

R. David O'Brien, CPA, Mosley, Pfundt & Glick Inc.

Greg Paxton, CAPS, CSP, Mr. Handyman of Kanawha Valley

John Piazza Sr., Piazza & Associates Consultants Inc.

Jeffrey Southard, South Haven Homes

Mike Stewart, Auspicious Homes

Michael Theunissen, Howling Hammer Builders Inc.

We also thank the following contributing writers and reviewers:

Alan Hanbury Jr., CAPS, CGP, CGR, GMR, House of Hanbury Builders Inc.

Steven W. Hays Sr., CPA, RubinBrown LLP

Bob Whitten, SMA Consulting

We thank those builders who provided valuable financial information for this 19th edition in *The Cost of Doing Business Study* series. Without their time and effort, this study would not have been possible.

NAHB strives to make *The Cost of Doing Business Study* a useful tool for understanding the home building industry and helping builders improve their businesses. If you have comments or suggestions for the next edition of the study, please contact NAHB's Business Management Department at 800-368-5242 x8388 or email mchilds@nahb.org.

Introduction

One of the best-kept secrets in a private company is typically the share of total revenue that stays in the company after paying all operating costs and expenses. For personal, business, or strategic reasons, that number – also known as net profit margin – tends to remain the purview of owner(s) and accountants. Other important metrics of a company's financial health, such as the ratio of current assets to current liabilities and the ratio of debt to equity, also remain undisclosed to outside parties. However, industries as a whole have a strong interest in understanding aggregate levels of profitability and measures of financial stability over time. For this reason, the National Association of Home Builders periodically conducts *The Cost of Doing Business Study*: a nationwide survey of single-family home building companies to produce profitability benchmarks for the industry.

The Cost of Doing Business Study is designed to provide "insider" information on how your business compares with similar types of home building companies as well as with the industry as a whole. The study reveals how much profit other builders and perhaps your competitors are earning to help you make informed decisions in setting profit goals. By providing up-to-date information on how various types of home building companies have fared recently, the book helps builders navigate an uncertain marketplace.

How the Study was Prepared

The Cost of Doing Business Study survey questionnaire was sent to more than 7,000 companies in April 2018. The questionnaire asked for 2017 financial and operational information as well as details about the type of single-family units closed in 2017. The analysis presented in *The Cost of Doing Business Study* is based only on responses from builders who reported their main operation to be single-family production or custom home building (either on owners' lots or builders' lots). NAHB received 105 responses. Not every question was answered by all respondents.

Organization of the Study

Nine chapters of study results and three related chapters comprise *The Cost of Doing Business Study, 2019 Edition*. The study is organized as follows:

Chapters 1–6 provide detailed information on gross profit, net profit, assets, liabilities, owner's equity, and financial ratios. Chapter 1 provides this information aggregated for all survey respondents, including a comparison between the top 25% and bottom 25% of builders. Subsequent chapters present the data for specific types of companies, such as small-volume and production builders.

Chapter 7 compares builders' performance by region (Midwest, South, and West) and business model (builders with land cost, without land cost, and combination builders). Chapter 8 provides data about the main operation of respondents, years in business, and number of units closed in 2017. Chapter 9 discusses historical trends based on data from *The Cost of Doing Business Study,* NAHB's construction costs surveys, and financial data available from public builders.

How to Use the Study

The Cost of Doing Business Study contains a wealth of information about the residential construction industry, but it is much more than a statistical report. Builders can use the study as a benchmark for their businesses by comparing their net profits to the net profits of other, similar building companies in their regions. A company's ability to generate adequate net profit strongly influences whether it will be successful. By sharing information about what comparable builders are earning, the study allows builders to analyze their financial performance, determine whether they are optimally managing their businesses, and assess whether they are achieving their business goals. The study helps company owners pinpoint areas for improvement, set budget targets, and create a road map for boosting profitability and increasing efficiency. The study breaks down survey findings by revenue, number of units closed, and whether builders have land costs. Where applicable, the study also shows results for the top and bottom quartiles (in terms of net profit performance). It also shows the average performance for all builders within a category (such as small builders). In addition, the study compares data from the most recent survey (2017 data) with the previous two surveys (2012 and 2014).

To get maximum value from this study, gather your financial information, including your income statement and balance sheet, and see how your performance compares.

Once you have made these comparisons, you can use the findings to make better business decisions and influence the behavior of others who impact your company's success or failure. For example, you can use the study as a selling point to lenders. If your company performs better than or even at the same level as the industry average, present these facts to negotiate better loan terms or interest rates.

Also use the findings to motivate your employees. For example, you can use industry averages as the basic performance level for rewarding employees with merit increases or bonuses.

Industry Profitability

In 2017, builders reported essentially the same gross profit margin as in 2014, but a higher net profit margin:

- The average gross profit rose from 18.9% in 2014 to 19.0% in 2017.
- The average net profit rose from 6.4% to 7.6% during the same period.

Gross profit equals sales minus the *cost of sales.* Cost of sales comprises

- materials and labor used in a home's construction;
- land on which the home is built; and
- indirect construction costs (field or construction expenses) that cannot be tied to a specific home.

Gross profit is measured before deducting operating expenses (financing, sales and marketing, general and administrative, depreciation, and owner's compensation). Here's how to calculate gross profit as a percentage of revenue:

1. Subtract the cost of sales from total sales (revenue).
2. Divide the gross profit by total sales (revenue).

The following example calculates gross profit margin for a company with $2,000,000 in total sales and $1,400,000 in cost of sales.

$2,000,000 − $1,400,000 = $600,000
$600,000 ÷ $2,000,000 = 0.30 or 30%

You can (and should) calculate gross profit at all operational levels — by home, by community, and for all jobs over the course of a year.

Net profit is the income from sales after deducting the cost of sales, expenses, and owner's compensation. In other words, net profit is the money a business earns after it has paid all the costs of both the project (hard costs) and the operating expenses (soft costs). When comparing your net profits with other builders or with overall industry performance, it is best to consider the pre-tax net profits, because many factors determine the taxes a business pays.

Consider the same company in which total sales are $2,000,000; *cost of sales,* or cost of goods sold, is $1,400,000; and operating expenses plus owner's compensation total $400,000. As described earlier, the gross profit is $600,000, a *gross margin* of 30%. Operating expenses take up 20% of total sales, leaving a net profit of $200,000, a net profit margin of 10%. To calculate the net profit as a percentage of sales, subtract the cost of sales, operating expenses, and owner's compensation from total sales, and then divide net profit by total sales as follows:

$2,000,000 − $1,400,000 − $400,000 = $200,000
$200,000 ÷ $2,000,000 = .1 or 10%.

Applying the Information to Your Business

How much profit should you be earning? Although there really is no ideal number, industry experts suggest aiming for gross profit margins of 22-27% and net profits of 8-15%. Although many companies post higher numbers, others do not achieve these levels. The averages presented in *The Cost of Doing Business Study* aren't necessarily appropriate goals for every company. To determine your profit goals, consider your level of risk, the cyclical nature of the industry, and the return you could get for your capital if you invested in another business sector or money market account.

Be cautious when considering changing your business plan based on information in this publication. Consider not only the benefits of the proposed change, but its costs. For example, although you could significantly increase your home sales price to increase your profit margin, that probably is not a realistic strategy for growing your bottom line. Because your homes probably would be too expensive for the market, your sales velocity would slow or stop.

Although *The Cost of Doing Business Study* is an essential resource to help you manage your business more effectively and profitably, you need other tools as well. Your annual operating budget helps you evaluate monthly financial performance. You also need tools to monitor construction quality, employee or trade contractor performance, schedules, and pre- and post-construction systems. When you measure performance in essential areas, you will have the information needed to improve management, quality, and profitability.

1

All Survey Respondents

Typically, one of the best-kept secrets in a private company is the share of total revenue that stays in the company after paying all operating costs and expenses. For a number of personal, business, or strategic reasons, that number — also known as net profit margin — tends to remain the purview of owner(s) and accountants. For similar motives, other important metrics of a company's financial health, such as the ratio of current assets to current liabilities and the ratio of debt to equity, remain undisclosed to outside parties. Despite these company-specific realities, however, industries as a whole have a strong interest in understanding aggregate levels of profitability and measures of financial stability over time. For this reason, the National Association of Home Builders periodically conducts *The Cost of Doing Business Study* — a nationwide survey of single-family home building companies designed to produce profitability benchmarks for the industry.

In all, more than 7,000 Builder members received the survey in April 2018, which asked for their company's income statement and balance sheet for 2017. The sample was stratified to accurately represent builders across the four Census regions of the country and also across builder size categories (in terms of number of single-family units built). A total of 105 responses were received, but not all questions were answered by every respondent.

The financial analysis presented throughout *The Cost of Doing Business Study* is based *solely* on responses from builders who reported their main operations to be single-family home building, whether production or custom (on the owner's or builder's lots). Table 1.1 breaks down the responses by U.S. Census region, type of builder, number of single-family homes closed in 2017, and total 2017 revenue.[1]

More than half of the study's respondents were in the South (54%), with similar shares coming from the Midwest (21%) and the West (20%), and a much smaller number from the Northeast (5%). This breakdown reasonably reflects the actual distribution of single-family housing starts in each region of the United States in 2017 (South: 53%; West: 24%; Midwest: 15%; and Northeast: 7%). The low response count from the Northeast (which is also the region with the fewest housing starts), however, made the findings for this region statistically unreliable, and as a result, the study omits analysis for the Northeast.

---

[1] Due to rounding, the numbers in the tables presented throughout the study may not add up to 100%.

When analyzed by type of builder, 40% of respondents were builders *with land costs* — defined in this study as those who only build speculative or pre-sold homes on lots they own. Another 40% were *combination* builders — defined as those who build homes on their own lots as well as their customers' lots. The remaining 21% were builders *without land costs* — defined as those who build exclusively on lots owned by their customers.

Table 1.1. Respondents' Profile

Region	% of Total
Northeast: Connecticut, Maine, Massachusetts, New Hampshire, New Jersey, New York, Pennsylvania, Rhode Island, Vermont	5
Midwest: Illinois, Indiana, Iowa, Kansas, Michigan, Minnesota, Missouri, Nebraska, North Dakota, Ohio, South Dakota, Wisconsin	21
South: Alabama, Arkansas, Delaware, District of Columbia, Florida, Georgia, Kentucky, Louisiana, Maryland, Mississippi, North Carolina, Oklahoma, South Carolina, Tennessee, Texas, Virginia, West Virginia	54
West: Alaska, Arizona, California, Colorado, Hawaii, Idaho, Montana, Nevada, New Mexico, Oregon, Utah, Washington, Wyoming	20
Type of Builder	**% of total**
With land costs	40
Without land costs	21
Combination	40
Single-Family Homes Closed in 2017	**% of total**
<10	40
10–25	22
26–99	22
≥100	16
Total 2017 Revenue	**% of total**
< $2 million	23
$2 to $9.9 million	36
$10 million+	40

For the purpose of this study, *small-volume* builders are those with 25 or fewer closings in 2017, and *production* builders are those with 26 or more closings. A total of 62% of all respondents were small-volume builders. Within that group, 40% closed fewer than 10 homes and 22% closed 10 to 25 homes. Of the 38% who were production builders, 22% closed 26 to 99 units and 16% closed 100 units or more.

During the housing recession of the late 2000s, the share of production builders responding to *The Cost of Doing Business Study* shrank significantly, going from 35% in 2006 to 18% in 2008. The return of more production builders to the last two editions of the study (35% in 2014 and 38% in 2017) is a reflection of the steady increase in residential construction seen in recent years (Single-family starts rose 80% between 2010 and 2017, going from 471,000 to 849,000 units).

The current distribution of responses by revenue is also indicative of higher levels of production in the home building industry. In 2014, 25% of builders responding reported total revenue under $2 million, while 40% reported between $2 million and $9.9 million. By 2017, those shares were down to 23% and 36%, respectively. In contrast, the share with $10 million or more in revenue rose from 35% in 2014 to 40% in 2017.

Balance Sheet and Income Statement

The Cost of Doing Business Study survey asked respondents for data from their 2017 income statement, including details about revenue, cost of sales and expenses. On the revenue side, the survey requested information about income generated from single-family and multifamily building, as well as from residential remodeling and light commercial/industrial building. In terms of cost of sales, builders were asked to provide land costs and both direct and indirect construction costs. Data on operating expenses were requested for financing expenses, sales and marketing expenses, general and administrative expenses, depreciation, and owner's compensation.

In addition to the income statement, the survey also inquired about builders' 2017 balance sheets: how much money was held in cash, how much in receivables and inventories, the amount tied to construction work in progress, as well as the amounts owed in current liabilities, construction loans, and long-term liabilities, along with the total amount held as owner's equity.

To provide historical context for the current findings, this study compares the 2017 data with results from the previous two editions of *The Cost of Doing Business Study* (covering 2012 and 2014). As Table 1.2 shows, total revenue for single-family builders in 2017 averaged

$16.4 million, which was barely 1% higher than the amount reported in 2014 ($16.2 million), but 20% more than in 2012 ($13.7 million). Despite recent gains in total revenue, builders' average revenue in 2017 was still 12% lower than in 2006, when it peaked at $18.7 million.

In 2017, all costs of sales combined averaged $13.3 million, taking up 81% of revenue — essentially the same share as in 2014 (81.1%). While most costs took up about the same share of revenue in 2017 as in 2014 (e.g., land costs accounted for 12.8% in 2014 and 12.6% in 2017), direct construction costs for single-family home building (which includes labor and material costs) rose to 62.7% — one whole percentage point higher than in 2014 (61.7%). After subtracting all costs of sales from revenue, the average gross profit stood at $3.1 million, or a 19% gross margin — again, essentially unchanged from 2014 (18.9%). Previous editions of this study reported gross margins

Table 1.2. Gross Profit

	2012		2014		2017	
	Average ($1,000s)	Share of revenue (%)	Average ($1,000s)	Share of revenue (%)	Average ($1,000s)	Share of revenue (%)
Revenue	13,693	100.0	16,233	100.0	16,429	100.0
Cost of sales						
Land costs	2,165	15.8	2,074	12.8	2,068	12.6
Direct costs: single-family	8,367	61.1	10,014	61.7	10,306	62.7
Direct costs: multifamily, remodeling, light commercial/industrial	260	1.9	416	2.6	425	2.6
Indirect construction costs	342	2.5	444	2.7	469	2.9
Other costs*	179	1.3	222	1.4	42	0.3
Total cost of sales	11,314	82.6	13,169	81.1	13,309	81.0
Gross profit	**2,380**	**17.4**	**3,064**	**18.9**	**3,120**	**19.0**

* This category includes the costs associated with the sale of land (raw or developed), trade-ins, repossessions, rental of investment property, parking facilities, and recreational facilities, construction management activities, design activities, and other unclassified construction activities.

of 20.8% in 2006, 14.4% in 2008, 15.3% in 2010, and 17.4% in 2012 (see Chapter 9).

Operating expenses in 2017 averaged $1.9 million, or 11.4% of builders' revenue — the lowest share in the history of the series, going back to 1970. In 2008, the least profitable year in the history of this survey (builders' net margin that year was -3%), operating expenses reached 17.4% of revenue. Strict belt-tightening on the part of builders has drastically cut this number since: down to 14.7% in 2010, 12.5% in both 2012 and 2014, and now to 11.4% in 2017.

Respondents spent smaller shares of revenue on every type of operating expense in 2017 than they did in 2014. Financing expenses' share of revenue declined from 1.4% to 1.3%, sales and marketing expenses went from 5% to 4.7%, and general and administrative (G&E) expenses fell from 4.7% to 4.1%. Even the share of revenue spent on owner's compensation saw a slight setback, slipping from 1.3% to 1.2% during this period. Meanwhile, depreciation was disaggregated from G&E expenses for the first time in 2017, and results show that a very minimal share of revenue (0.1%) was spent on it.

Lower operating expenses allowed builders to post an average net profit margin of 7.6% ($1.2 million) in 2017, the highest margin in this study since 2006 (7.7%). This result marks the fourth consecutive increase in builders' average net profit margin in this series, rising from -3% in 2006, to 0.5% in 2010, 4.9% in 2012, and 6.4% in 2014. The highest net profit margin ever reported in this survey was 10% in 1991. Figure 1.1 summarizes builders' income statements for 2017.

In addition to the income statement, *The Cost of Doing Business Study* has tracked the balance sheet of single-family builders over time. As Table 1.4 shows, builders responding to the survey had total assets averaging $8 million in 2017, down about 12% from 2014 ($9.2 million) and 10% from 2010 ($8.9 million)[2]. The majority of builders' assets in 2017 were tied to construction work in progress ($5.2 million or 64.2% of all assets), another $626,000 was held in cash (7.8%), $588,000 was in receivables

---

[2] *The Cost of Doing Business Study* is not designed as a longitudinal survey tracking the same companies over time. Instead, each year's study is based on responses from independent samples of current members of NAHB.

Table 1.3. Net Profit

	2012		2014		2017	
	Average ($1,000s)	Share of revenue (%)	Average ($1,000s)	Share of revenue (%)	Average ($1,000s)	Share of revenue (%)
Gross profit	2,380	17.4	3,064	18.9	3,120	19.0
Operating expenses						
Financing expenses	227	1.7	225	1.4	220	1.3
Sales & mktg. expenses	696	5.1	817	5.0	779	4.7
General & administrative expenses	685	5.0	766	4.7	666	4.1
Depreciation	n/a	n/a	n/a	n/a	19	0.1
Owner's compensation	106	0.8	215	1.3	194	1.2
Total operating expenses	1,714	12.5	2,023	12.5	1,879	11.4
Net profit (loss)	666	4.9	1,040	6.4	1,241	7.6

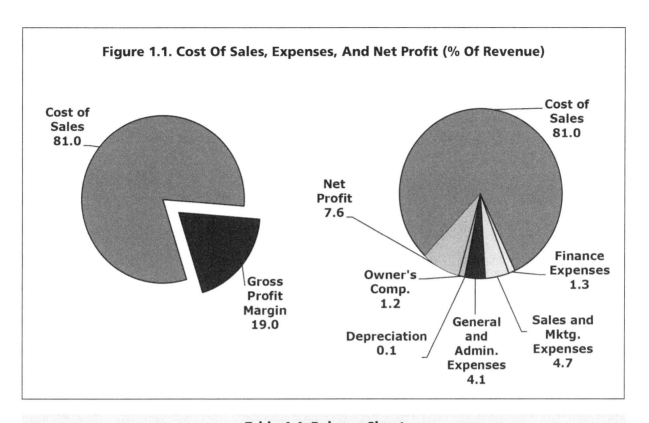

Figure 1.1. Cost Of Sales, Expenses, And Net Profit (% Of Revenue)

Table 1.4. Balance Sheet

	2012		2014		2017	
	Average ($1,000s)	Share of total (%)	Average ($1,000s)	Share of total (%)	Average ($1,000s)	Share of total (%)
Assets						
Current assets						
Cash	631	7.1	645	7.1	626	7.8
Receivables & inventories	n/a	n/a	n/a	n/a	588	7.3
Construction work in progress	6,013	67.3	6,270	68.5	5,155	64.2
Other current assets	1,365	15.3	1,274	13.9	907	11.3
Total current assets	8,008	89.7	8,189	89.5	7,276	90.6
Other assets	922	10.3	963	10.5	758	9.4
Total assets	8,930	100.0	9,152	100.0	8,034	100.0
Liabilities						
Current liabilities	1,826	20.4	1,917	20.9	1,869	23.3
Construction loans payable	3,011	33.7	3,169	34.6	2,611	32.5
Total current liabilities	4,838	54.2	5,086	55.6	4,480	55.8
Long-term loans payable	n/a	n/a	n/a	n/a	749	9.3
Other long-term liabilities	844	9.4	1,087	11.9	58	0.7
Total liabilities	5,681	63.6	6,173	67.4	5,287	65.8
Owner's equity	3,249	36.4	2,979	32.6	2,747	34.2
Total liabilities & owner's equity	8,930	100.0	9,152	100.0	8,034	100.0

and inventories (7.3%), $907,000 in other current assets (11.3%), and $758,000 was tied to other assets (9.4%).

On the liabilities side, respondents owed an average of $5.3 million in 2017, about 14% less than in 2014 ($6.2 million) and 7% less than in 2012 ($5.7 million). While current liabilities represented 55.8% of all assets, practically the same as in 2014 (55.6%), long-term liabilities decreased to 10% from 11.9% in 2014. This fall in long-term liabilities led the share of assets financed through debt to decline to 65.8% in 2017, which is lower than in 2014 (67.4%) but higher than in 2012 (63.6%).

While the amount of money builders held as equity in their businesses (i.e. capital investment) declined from $3 million to $2.7 million from 2014 to 2017, the share of assets financed through equity actually increased. In 2014, equity represented 32.6% of builders' assets; by 2017, that share grew to 34.2%.

The current ratio is a liquidity measure that evaluates a company's ability to repay its short-term liabilities using its short-term assets. It is calculated by dividing current assets by current liabilities, and in general, the higher the current ratio, the healthier the financial state of a company. In 2017, the current ratio for all single-family home builders responding to the survey was 1.62, or in other words, builders had 62% more current assets than current liabilities. This ratio was essentially the same as in 2014 (1.61), somewhat lower than in 2012 (1.66), but much higher than a decade ago: 1.43 in 2006 and 1.45 in 2008.

Another important gauge of a company's financial health is its debt-to-equity ratio. Calculated by dividing total liabilities by total equity, this ratio measures the level of leverage, and therefore risk, in a company. In 2017, build-ers reported an average debt-to-equity ratio of 1.92, which is interpreted as having 92% more debt than equity in their businesses. This ratio declined since 2014 (2.07), demonstrating that builders' reliance on debt to run their businesses receded in 2017. As a point of reference, builders' debt-to-equity ratio reached 2.80 in 2006, a signal of the significant levels of risk taken during the housing boom. As a broader reference, a debt-to-equity ratio above 4.0 is considered so risky that most financial institutions would likely turn down additional borrowing requests from any company with that level of debt.

Two additional ratios, return on assets (ROA) and return on equity (ROE), show how effectively a company is using its assets and invested capital to churn out profits. In 2017, builders' ROA stood at 15.4%, an important improvement over 2014 (11.4%) and 2012 (7.5%). In comparison, builders' ROA in 2008 was -2.7% and barely positive in 2010 (0.6%). Meanwhile, builders reported an impressive 45.2% ROE in 2017, far ahead of the 34.9% reported in 2014 or the 20.5% in 2012. Again in comparison, builders' ROE in 2008 was -8.4% and barely positive in 2010 (1.9%).

Table 1.5. Financial Ratios

	2012	2014	2017
Current ratio	1.66	1.61	1.62
Debt-to-equity ratio	1.75	2.07	1.92
Return on assets	7.5%	11.4%	15.4%
Return on equity	20.5%	34.9%	45.2%

Top and Bottom 25%

When looking at profitability benchmarks, it is important to look at averages across the industry, but it is just as critical to understand how the most and least successful quartiles of builders performed. This section, therefore, shows results tabulated separately for two groups of respondents: those in the top 25% in terms of net profit margins and those in the bottom 25% (Appendix V.2.).

Total revenue among builders in the top 25% group averaged $29.5 million in 2017. Cost of sales took up $23.0 million (77.9%) of that amount, leaving an average of $6.5 million in gross profit, a 22.1% gross profit margin. After subtracting $3.2 million (10.7%) in operating expenses, their average net profit was $3.4 million, a net margin of 11.4% (Figure 1.2).

Among builders in the bottom 25%, total revenue in 2017 averaged $7.7 million. Cost of sales accounted for $6.6 million (86.1%) of that, leaving $1.1 million in gross profits, for an average 13.9% gross profit margin. After deducting $984,000 (12.8%) in operating expenses, this least successful group had a net profit of $82,000, a net margin of 1.1%. This is only the second time the bottom 25% group

has had a positive net profit since 2002, when results for the top and bottom quartiles began to be produced. The first time was in 2014 (0.9%).

Because the line between the owner's compensation and the business' profit can be blurry in many companies (especially small ones), it is useful to analyze a broader measure of performance that combines the share of revenue spent on owner's compensation and the net profit margin. As Figure 1.2 shows, this overall measure of profitability was 8.8% for all builders combined, 12.5% for the top 25%, and 2.5% for the bottom 25%.

For many years, even this broader measure of performance was negative for the bottom 25% group, going as low as -20.3% in 2008. Among builders in the top 25%, overall profitability declined after the housing recession as well, but never sank below 10%, bottoming out at 10.6% in 2010.

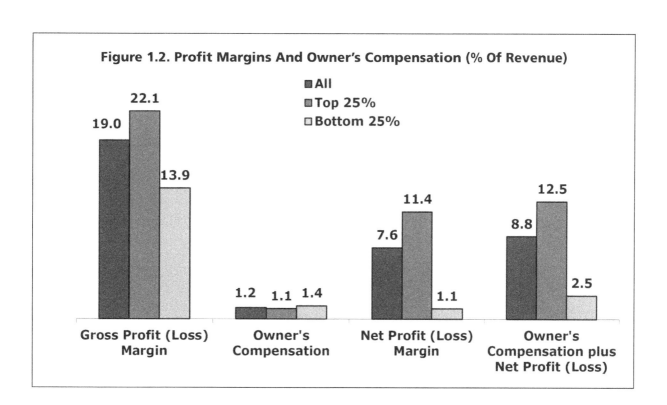

Figure 1.2. Profit Margins And Owner's Compensation (% Of Revenue)

The 2017 balance sheet for the top 25% of respondents shows they had an average of $16 million in total assets, $9.4 million in liabilities, and $6.6 million in owner's equity. On the other hand, builders in the bottom 25% had about one-third the amount of assets ($5.6 million), owner's equity ($2.4 million), and total liabilities ($3.3 million). Table 1.6 summarizes important statistics from the income statement and balance sheet for the top and bottom 25% of respondents.

Builders in the top 25% saw net profit margins remain rather flat for a second consecutive study: 11.4% in 2017, compared to 11.1% in 2012 and 11% in 2014. In addition, and largely due to rising liabilities, this group's current ratio and debt-to-equity ratio deteriorated between 2014 and 2017: The current ratio

declined from 2.61 to 1.84 while the debt-to-equity ratio increased from 0.74 to 1.41. The ROE for the top 25% was an impressive 50.8% in 2017, meaning that these builders produced revenue equivalent to about half their invested capital!

The net profit margin for builders in the bottom 25%, meanwhile, posted a second consecutive improvement, going from -4.7% in 2012, to 0.9% in 2014, and 1.1% in 2017. Exactly the opposite result as their top 25% counterparts, this group saw its average current ratio and debt-to-equity ratio both improve significantly from 2014 to 2017, driven by a dramatic decline in liabilities: The current ratio jumped from 1.63 to 2.29, while the debt-to-equity ratio fell from 12.65 to 1.39. The ROE for the bottom 25% in 2017 was only 3.5%, however.

Table 1.6. Top and Bottom 25%

	2012		2014		2017	
	Top 25%	**Bottom 25%**	**Top 25%**	**Bottom 25%**	**Top 25%**	**Bottom 25%**
Gross profit (loss) margin (%)	22.60	10.90	22.50	13.20	22.10	13.90
Net profit (loss) margin (%)	11.10	(4.70)	11.00	0.90	11.40	1.10
Total assets (millions $)	8.13	6.66	11.75	6.87	15.97	5.63
Owner's equity (millions $)	3.99	1.87	6.76	0.50	6.61	2.36
Current ratio	2.00	1.45	2.61	1.63	1.84	2.29
Debt-to-equity ratio	1.04	2.56	0.74	12.65	1.41	1.39
Return on assets (%)	18.30	(3.40)	19.30	1.00	21.10	1.50
Return on equity (%)	37.20	(12.10)	33.50	13.80	50.80	3.50

2

Builders With Land Costs

Builders with land costs (those that *only* build spec or pre-sold homes on their own lots) responding to *The Cost of Doing Business Study* in 2017 had smaller — yet much more profitable — operations than similar types of builders in previous editions of this survey: Their total revenue averaged $14.7 million, compared to a much higher $20.5 million in 2014 and $18.2 million in 2012 (Table 2.1). Cost of sales averaged $11.7 million, or 79.1% of all revenue, leaving a gross profit of $3.1 million, for a 20.9% gross profit margin. The latter was higher than in both 2014 (18.4%) and 2012 (18.9%). In fact, 2017's gross margin among

builders with land costs was the highest for this type of builder since 2006 (22.1%).

Among the three types of business models analyzed in this study — builders with land costs, without land costs, and combination builders — those with land costs achieved a higher gross profit margin in 2017 (20.9%) than combination builders (17.2%) or builders without land costs (15.3%) (Appendix V.1.).

On a net basis, builders with land costs lost money in 2008 (-4.9%) and 2010 (-1%), in large part due to running their businesses with

Table 2.1 Gross Profit

	2012		2014		2017	
	Average ($1,000s)	Share of revenue (%)	Average ($1,000s)	Share of revenue (%)	Average ($1,000s)	Share of revenue (%)
Revenue	18,249	100.0	20,453	100.0	14,726	100.0
Cost of sales						
Land costs	2,989	16.4	3,275	16.0	2,547	17.3
Direct costs: single-family	11,025	60.4	12,132	59.3	8,103	55.0
Direct costs: multifamily, remodeling, light commercial/industrial	76	0.4	301	1.5	629	4.3
Indirect construction costs	430	2.4	527	2.6	363	2.5
Other costs	287	1.6	458	2.2	10	0.1
Total cost of sales	14,806	81.1	16,694	81.6	11,652	79.1
Gross profit	**3,443**	**18.9**	**3,758**	**18.4**	**3,074**	**20.9**

operating expenses that exceeded 18% of their total revenue. After reining in and lowering all these expenses to around 12.5%, they returned to profitability in 2012 and 2014, posting net margins of around 6% (Table 2.2). Data for 2017 show that builders with land costs managed to do it again: They reduced operating expenses to only 10.6% of revenue. G&E expenses, for example, fell from 4.2% of revenue in 2014 to 3.4% in 2017, while owner's compensation was reduced from 1.5% to 1.0%.

In all, builders with land costs posted an average net profit of $1.5 million for 2017, achieving a record-high net profit margin of 10.3%. That was the best financial performance by this type of builder since 2006, when they reported a net margin of 9.1%. Figure 2.1 summarizes the income statement for builders with land costs for 2017.

As mentioned earlier, builders with land costs who responded to the latest *The Cost of Doing Business Study* are significantly smaller companies than in earlier editions of the survey. In fact, their total assets averaged only $8.6 million in 2017, much lower than in 2012 ($12.1 million) or 2014 ($13.6 million). About $686,000 of their assets in 2017 (8% of the total) was held in cash, another $674,000 in receivables and inventories (7.8%), $5.3 million in construction work in progress (61.2%), $636,000 in other current assets (such as refundable deposits and furnished model homes) (7.4%), and $1.4 million in other (non-current) assets (15.6%) (Table 2.3).

On the liabilities side of the ledger, builders with land costs ended 2017 with $5.6 million in total debt, about half the size of their debt in 2014 ($10.2 million). As a result, this group of builders financed a significantly smaller share of their assets through debt in 2017 (64.4%) than in 2014 (75.1%). Meanwhile, average owner's equity stood at $3.1 million, 9% lower than in 2014. In the end, invested capital financed 35.6% of all assets for builders with land costs in 2017, a considerably higher share than in 2014 (24.9%) and closer to where it stood in 2012 (36.8%).

Table 2.2. Net Profit

	2012		2014		2017	
	Average ($1,000s)	Share of revenue (%)	Average ($1,000s)	Share of revenue (%)	Average ($1,000s)	Share of revenue (%)
Gross profit	3,443	18.9	3,758	18.4	3,074	20.9
Operating expenses						
Financing expenses	299	1.6	393	1.9	233	1.6
Sales & mktg. expenses	1,014	5.6	1,012	4.9	670	4.5
General & administrative expenses	916	5.0	849	4.2	493	3.4
Depreciation	n/a	n/a	n/a	n/a	11	0.1
Owner's compensation	75	0.4	299	1.5	153	1.0
Total operating expenses	2,304	12.6	2,552	12.5	1,559	10.6
Net profit (loss)	1,139	6.2	1,206	5.9	1,514	10.3

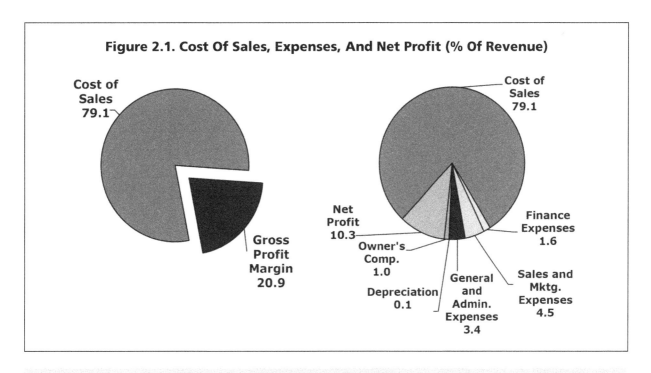

Figure 2.1. Cost Of Sales, Expenses, And Net Profit (% Of Revenue)

Table 2.3. Balance Sheet

	2012		2014		2017	
	Average ($1,000s)	Share of total (%)	Average ($1,000s)	Share of total (%)	Average ($1,000s)	Share of total (%)
Assets						
Current assets						
Cash	1,014	8.4	955	7.0	686	8.0
Receivables & Inventories	n/a	n/a	n/a	n/a	674	7.8
Construction work in progress	8,516	70.3	9,109	67.0	5,282	61.2
Other current assets	1,919	15.8	1,994	14.7	636	7.4
Total current assets	11,450	94.5	12,057	88.7	7,278	84.4
Other assets	668	5.5	1,538	11.3	1,350	15.6
Total assets	**12,118**	**100.0**	**13,594**	**100.0**	**8,628**	**100.0**
Liabilities						
Current liabilities	2,758	22.8	2,826	20.8	1,042	12.1
Construction loans payable	4,388	36.2	5,010	36.9	3,393	39.3
Total current liabilities	7,147	59.0	7,835	57.6	4,434	51.4
Long-term loans payable	n/a	n/a	n/a	n/a	1,010	11.7
Other long-term liabilities	510	4.2	2,372	17.4	108	1.3
Total liabilities	**7,657**	**63.2**	**10,207**	**75.1**	**5,553**	**64.4**
Owner's equity	**4,461**	**36.8**	**3,387**	**24.9**	**3,075**	**35.6**
Total liabilities & owner's equity	**12,118**	**100.0**	**13,594**	**100.0**	**8,628**	**100.0**

Lower levels of debt among builders with land costs had a noticeable impact on the group's financial ratios. The current ratio grew from 1.54 in 2014 to 1.64 in 2017, while the debt-to-equity ratio dropped from 3.01 to 1.81 (meaning they went from holding 3.01 times more debt than equity to only 1.81 times). Finally, builders with land costs effectively increased the profitability of their assets and invested capital: ROA rose to 17.6% (from 8.9% in 2014) and ROE increased to 49.2% (from 35.6%) (Table 2.4).

Table 2.4. Financial Ratios

	2012	2014	2017
Current ratio	1.60	1.54	1.64
Debt-to-equity ratio	1.72	3.01	1.81
Return on assets (%)	9.40	8.90	17.6
Return on equity (%)	25.50	35.60	49.2

Note: No data for the top and bottom 25% of builders with land costs were produced because of insufficient sample size.

3

Builders Without Land Costs

Unlike their counterparts *with* land costs, builders *without* land costs (those that build exclusively on their customers' land) reported an increase in total revenue for 2017, coming in at $6.1 million. That was 23% higher than the previous series-high of $4.9 million reported in both 2006 and 2014. Cost of sales ($5.1 million) took up 84.7% of all revenue, a smaller share than in 2014 (86.4%), and therefore, the gross profit margin rose to 15.3% ($931,000) — ahead of the 13.6% posted in 2014 and, in fact, the highest this group has seen since 2008 (19.4%).

The share of revenue that builders without land costs spent on operating expenses saw about a one percentage point increase from 2014 to 2017, rising from 10.2% to 11.1% (Table 3.2). Most of that gain stemmed from higher G&E expenses, which went from 6.4% to 7.2% (including depreciation). Ultimately, this group of builders posted a net profit of $258,000, or 4.3% of revenue — an improvement over 2014 (3.6%) and also, the highest net margin this group has seen since 2008 (5.1%). Figure 3.1 summarizes the income statement for builders without land costs for 2017.

Table 3.1. Gross Profit

	2012		2014		2017	
	Average ($1,000s)	Share of revenue (%)	Average ($1,000s)	Share of revenue (%)	Average ($1,000s)	Share of revenue (%)
Revenue	3,485	100.0	4,931	100.0	6,076	100.0
Cost of sales						
Land costs	0	0.0	0	0.0	0	0.0
Direct costs: single-family	2,246	64.5	3,276	66.4	4,787	78.8
Direct costs: multifamily, remodeling, light commercial/industrial	579	16.6	624	12.7	184	3.0
Indirect construction costs	72	2.1	167	3.4	103	1.7
Other costs	84	2.4	191	3.9	72	1.2
Total cost of sales	2,981	85.6	4,258	86.4	5,145	84.7
Gross profit	**503**	**14.4**	**673**	**13.6**	**931**	**15.3**

Table 3.2. Net Profit

	2012		2014		2017	
	Average ($1,000s)	Share of revenue (%)	Average ($1,000s)	Share of revenue (%)	Average ($1,000s)	Share of revenue (%)
Gross profit	503	14.4	673	13.6	931	15.3
Operating expenses						
Financing expenses	8	0.2	7	0.2	7	0.1
Sales & mktg. expenses	27	0.8	34	0.7	38	0.6
General & administrative expenses	221	6.3	314	6.4	426	7.0
Depreciation	n/a	n/a	n/a	n/a	11	0.2
Owner's compensation	101	2.9	141	2.9	191	3.1
Total operating expenses	358	10.2	496	10.2	673	11.1
Net profit (loss)	146	4.2	176	3.6	258	4.3

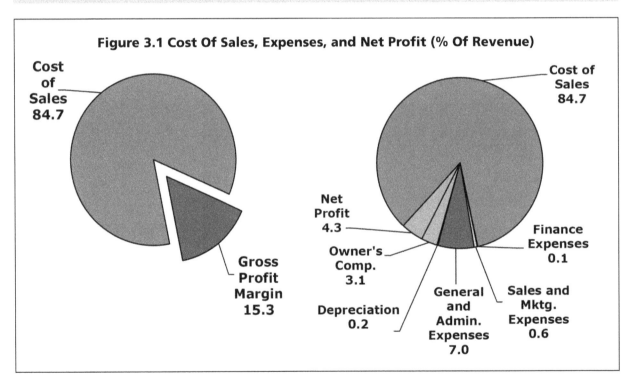

Figure 3.1 Cost Of Sales, Expenses, and Net Profit (% Of Revenue)

In 2006, builders without land costs reported an average of $1.9 million in total assets, yet by 2012, after the housing recession, that number had shrunk to $770,000. In 2017, this type of builder reported an average of $1.4 million in total assets, slightly ahead of the $1.3 million held in 2014. Their largest category of assets was receivables and inventories, at $441,000 (32.6% of all assets), followed by construc-tion work in progress (31.9%). Overall, cur-rent assets rose from representing 81.2% of all assets in 2014 to 90.8% in 2017 (Table 3.3).

In sharp contrast to assets (which grew 3%), builders without land costs drove their total liabilities down by 32%, going from $980,000 in 2014 to $668,000 in 2017. Both current and long-term liabilities saw significant reductions

Table 3.3. Balance Sheet

	2012		2014		2017	
	Average ($1,000s)	Share of total (%)	Average ($1,000s)	Share of total (%)	Average ($1,000s)	Share of total (%)
Assets						
Current assets						
Cash	131	17.0	214	16.3	307	22.7
Receivables and Inventories	n/a	n/a	n/a	n/a	441	32.6
Construction work in progress	233	30.3	451	34.3	432	31.9
Other current assets	320	41.6	403	30.6	48	3.6
Total current assets	684	88.9	1,068	81.2	1,229	90.8
Other assets	85	11.1	248	18.8	125	9.2
Total assets	770	100.0	1,316	100.0	1,353	100.0
Liabilities						
Current liabilities	367	47.6	744	56.5	559	41.3
Construction loans payable	46	6.0	32	2.5	71	5.3
Total current liabilities	412	53.6	777	59.0	630	46.5
Long-term loans payable	n/a	n/a	n/a	n/a	23	1.7
Other long-term liabilities	89	11.5	204	15.5	15	1.1
Total liabilities	501	65.1	980	74.5	668	49.4
Owner's equity	268	34.9	335	25.5	685	50.6
Total liabilities & owner's equity	770	100.0	1,316	100.0	1,353	100.0

during this period, and together accounted for only 49.4% of all assets, compared to 74.5% in 2014! This means that more than half of all assets held by this type of builder in 2017 (50.6%) were financed through equity, twice the share in 2014 (25.5%).

Falling current liabilities allowed the current ratio for builders without land costs to grow to 1.95 in 2017, the highest it has been since 2010 (3.69). Lower overall debt levels and higher capital investments led the debt-to-equity ratio to fall below 1 (to 0.97) in 2017, which indicates this group of builders is running their businesses with lower levels of risk than in recent years (the ratio was 2.92 in 2014

and 1.87 in 2012). Meanwhile, ROA improved to 19.1% (from 13.4% in 2014), while ROE was 37.7% (lower than the 52.6% reported in 2014).

Table 3.4. Financial Ratios

	2012	2014	2017
Current ratio	1.66	1.38	1.95
Debt-to-equity ratio	1.87	2.92	0.97
Return on assets (%)	18.90	13.40	19.1
Return on equity (%)	54.20	52.60	37.7

Note: No data for the top and bottom 25% of builders without land costs were produced because of insufficient sample size.

4

Combination Builders

Total revenue for combination builders (those who build homes on their own land but also on their customers' lots) averaged $19.9 million in 2017, 29% higher than in 2014 ($15.4 million), and in fact, the highest level seen since 2006 ($27.6 million) (Table 4.1). The most important change in their cost structure in 2017 was the substantial increase in the share of revenue spent on direct construction costs (i.e., construction labor, material, and subcontractors) to build single-family homes, which rose to 67% from 60.5% in 2014. All together, the share of revenue spent on all items under cost of sales rose to 82.8% in 2017 (from 80.5% in 2014), and as a result, the net profit margin slipped to 17.2% (from 19.5%).

In absolute dollar terms, combination builders posted an average net profit of $3.4 million, 14% higher than in 2014 ($3 million).

Despite seeing their costs of sales rise in 2017, combination builders managed to keep operating expenses in check, staying at 11.9% of revenue — the same share as in 2014 (Table 4.2). After subtracting operating expenses from gross profit, these builders posted a $1.1 million net profit, resulting in the second strongest net profit margin (5.3%) combination builders have seen since records began to be kept in 2002 (the highest was 7.6% in 2014). Figure 4.1 summarizes the income statement for combination builders for 2017.

Table 4.1. Gross Profit

	2012		2014		2017	
	Average ($1,000s)	Share of revenue (%)	Average ($1,000s)	Share of revenue (%)	Average ($1,000s)	Share of revenue (%)
Revenue	17,458	100.0	15,437	100.0	19,917	100.0
Cost of sales						
Land costs	3,061	17.5	2,143	13.9	2,060	10.3
Direct costs: single-family	10,760	61.6	9,337	60.5	13,344	67.0
Direct costs: multifamily, remodeling, light commercial/industrial	203	1.2	423	2.7	380	1.9
Indirect construction costs	475	2.7	472	3.1	641	3.2
Other costs	146	0.8	48	0.3	59	0.3
Total cost of sales	14,645	83.9	12,424	80.5	16,483	82.8
Gross profit	2,813	16.1	3,013	19.5	3,434	17.2

Table 4.2. Net Profit

	2012		2014		2017	
	Average ($1,000s)	Share of revenue (%)	Average ($1,000s)	Share of revenue (%)	Average ($1,000s)	Share of revenue (%)
Gross profit	2,813	16.1	3,013	19.5	3,434	17.2
Operating expenses						
Financing expenses	335	1.9	204	1.3	228	1.1
Sales & mktg. expenses	902	5.2	806	5.2	1,027	5.2
General & administrative expenses	820	4.7	644	4.2	901	4.5
Depreciation	n/a	n/a	n/a	n/a	28	0.1
Owner's compensation	129	0.7	184	1.2	186	0.9
Total operating expenses	2,186	12.5	1,838	11.9	2,370	11.9
Net profit (loss)	627	3.6	1,175	7.6	1,064	5.3

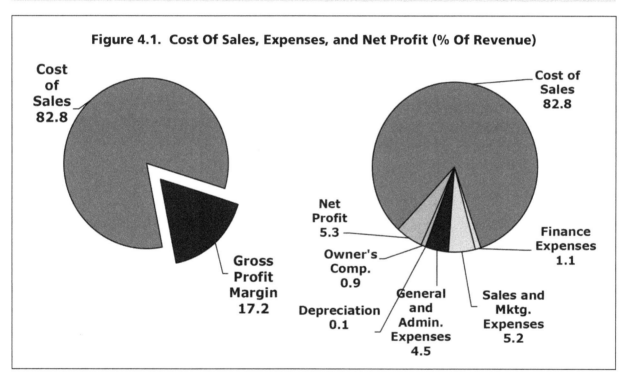

Figure 4.1. Cost Of Sales, Expenses, and Net Profit (% Of Revenue)

The balance sheet for the average combination builder was smaller in 2017 ($8.5 million in assets) than in 2014 ($9.4 million) or 2012 ($11.2 million). The last time their assets were lower was in 2010, when they were only $4.8 million. A breakdown by type of asset shows that in 2017 $6.3 million (73.6% of all assets) was tied up to construction work in progress, $608,000 in other (fixed) assets (7.1%), and

only $469,000 in cash (5.5%). In the end, 92.9% of all assets were current assets, essentially the same share as in 2014 (92.8%) (Table 4.3).

In contrast to the decline in total assets, combination builders saw liabilities increase from 2014 to 2017. Of particular note is the rise in current liabilities, which went from 16.8% ($1.6 million) of all assets to 35.8% ($3.1 mil-

Table 4.3. Balance Sheet

	2012		2014		2017	
	Average ($1,000s)	Share of total (%)	Average ($1,000s)	Share of total (%)	Average ($1,000s)	Share of total (%)
Assets						
Current assets						
Cash	633	5.6	592	6.3	469	5.5
Receivables and inventories	n/a	n/a	n/a	n/a	583	6.8
Construction work in progress	7,443	66.3	6,954	74.2	6,279	73.6
Other current assets	1,614	14.4	1,155	12.3	589	6.9
Total current assets	9,689	86.3	8,701	92.8	7,920	92.9
Other assets	1,536	13.7	676	7.2	608	7.1
Total assets	**11,225**	**100.0**	**9,377**	**100.0**	**8,528**	**100.0**
Liabilities						
Current liabilities	1,974	17.6	1,579	16.8	3,050	35.8
Construction loans payable	3,726	33.2	3,493	37.3	2,414	28.3
Total current liabilities	5,700	50.8	5,072	54.1	5,464	64.1
Long-term loans payable	n/a	n/a	n/a	n/a	526	6.2
Other long-term liabilities	1,652	14.7	569	6.1	40	0.5
Total liabilities	**7,352**	**65.5**	**5,641**	**60.2**	**6,031**	**70.7**
Owner's equity	**3,873**	**34.5**	**3,736**	**39.8**	**2,497**	**29.3**
Total liabilities & owner's equity	**11,225**	**100.0**	**9,377**	**100.0**	**8,528**	**100.0**

lion). In all, total debt (current + long-term) for combination builders averaged $6 million in 2017, up from $5.6 million in 2014. As a result, the share of their assets financed through liabilities jumped from 60.2% to 70.7% during this period, while owner's equity fell from $3.7 million (39.8% of assets) to $2.5 million (29.3%).

Considerably higher levels of debt, both current and long term, caused the deterioration of some financial ratios for combination builders in 2017. For example, the current ratio (which again measures liquidity, or the ability to repay current liabilities with current assets) fell to 1.45, after staying around 1.70 in both 2012 and 2014. The debt-to-equity ratio (which measures leverage levels) also moved into riskier territory, rising from 1.51 in 2014 to 2.42 in

2017, and indicating that combination builders owed 2.42 times the amount of equity in their books. Meanwhile, ROA was unchanged, remaining at 12.5%, but ROE improved to 42.6% from 31.4% in 2014 (Table 4.4).

Table 4.4. Financial Ratios

	2012	2014	2017
Current ratio	1.70	1.72	1.45
Debt-to-equity ratio	1.90	1.51	2.42
Return on assets (%)	5.60	12.50	12.50
Return on equity (%)	16.20	31.40	42.60

Note: No data for the top and bottom 25% of combination builders were produced because of insufficient sample size.

5

Small-Volume Builders

All Small-Volume Builders Combined

For the purpose of this study, a small-volume builder is one that closes 25 or fewer units per year. According to the 2017 NAHB Builder Member Census, approximately 81% of our association's Builder members fall into this classification. Total revenue for the typical small-volume builder in 2017 was $4.4 million, about 5% lower than in 2014 ($4.6 million), but 33% higher than in 2012 ($3.3 million). Despite increases in land costs and direct construction costs for single-family building in 2017, all together costs of sales accounted for 83.2% of revenue, essentially the same share as

in 2014 (83.6%). That left $737,000 as gross profit, a 16.8% gross margin — slightly ahead of 2014 (16.4%) and the highest reported by this group since 2006 (16.9%) (Table 5.1).

Small-volume builders spent an average of $486,000 on operating expenses in 2017. Nearly half of that amount paid for G&E expenses ($229,000 or 5.2% of revenue), followed by compensation to the owner ($118,000 or 2.7% of revenue). All combined, operating expenses usd 11% of total revenue, just below the 11.3% reported in 2014 (Table 5.2). In the end, small-volume builders posted a net profit margin of 5.7% ($251,000) — the best in this

Table 5.1. Gross profit

	2012		2014		2017	
	Average ($1,000s)	Share of revenue (%)	Average ($1,000s)	Share of revenue (%)	Average ($1,000s)	Share of revenue (%)
Revenue	3,308	100.0	4,628	100.0	4,400	100.0
Cost of Sales						
Land costs	221	6.7	277	6.0	347	7.9
Direct costs: single-family	2,160	65.3	2,899	62.6	2,973	67.6
Direct costs: multifamily, remodeling, light commercial/industrial	347	10.5	459	9.9	217	4.9
Indirect construction costs	83	2.5	129	2.8	119	2.7
Other costs	43	1.3	106	2.3	6	0.1
Total cost of Sales	2,854	86.3	3,871	83.6	3,662	83.2
Gross Profit	454	13.7	757	16.4	737	16.8

group's history going back to 2002. It is important to point out that the net margin for small builders has been growing steadily in recent years: from -1.4% in 2008, to 1.9% in 2010, 4.0% in 2012, and to 5.0% in 2014. Figure 5.1 summarizes the income statement for small-volume builders for 2017 (Appendix V.3.).

Small-volume builders substantially contracted the size of their balance sheets in 2017, with total assets averaging only $1.8 million, 24% lower than in 2014 ($2.3 million). Current assets (cash, receivables and inventories, construction work in progress, and other current assets) declined both in absolute terms (from

Table 5.2. Net Profit

	2012		2014		2017	
	Average ($1,000s)	Share of revenue (%)	Average ($1,000s)	Share of revenue (%)	Average ($1,000s)	Share of revenue (%)
Gross profit	454	13.7	757	16.4	737	16.8
Operating expenses						
Financing expenses	25	0.7	40	0.9	30	0.7
Sales & mktg. expenses	57	1.7	92	2.0	104	2.4
General & administrative expenses	175	5.3	268	5.8	229	5.2
Depreciation	n/a	n/a	n/a	n/a	5	0.1
Owner's compensation	66	2.0	125	2.7	118	2.7
Total operating expenses	322	9.7	525	11.3	486	11.0
Net profit (loss)	132	4.0	232	5.0	251	5.7

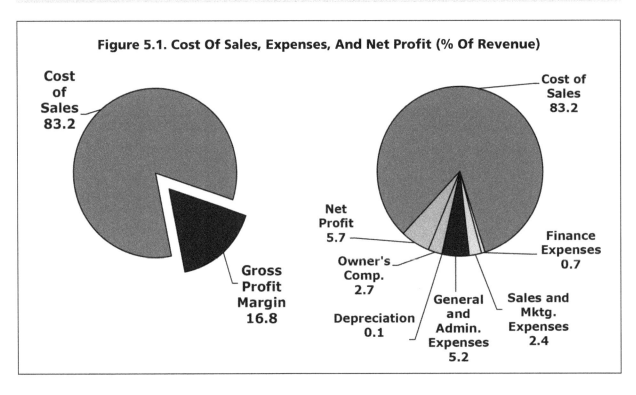

Figure 5.1. Cost Of Sales, Expenses, And Net Profit (% Of Revenue)

Cost of Sales 83.2

Gross Profit Margin 16.8

Cost of Sales 83.2

Net Profit 5.7

Owner's Comp. 2.7

Depreciation 0.1

General and Admin. Expenses 5.2

Sales and Mktg. Expenses 2.4

Finance Expenses 0.7

$2 million to $1.3 million) and as a share of all assets (from 83.6% to 72.3%), while fixed assets grew in relevance from 16.4% to 27.7%.

The severe decline in assets among small-volume builders in 2017 went hand in hand with the dramatic fall in liabilities, which were cut 53% from $1.6 million (2014) to $770,000 (2017). All types of debt declined during this period, but current liabilities dropped the most, going from $1.3 million to only $615,000. In the end, small builders' reliance on debt to finance their businesses was significantly reduced, as only 42.9% of their assets were backed up by debt (vs. 69.9% in 2014) (Table 5.3). Instead, these builders increased the amount of invested capital from an average of $706,000 to $1 million during this period,

driving the share of assets financed by equity up from 30.1% to 57.1%.

The drastic reduction of liabilities in 2017 improved the financial health of the typical small-volume builder, demonstrated by changes to their financial ratios. The current ratio, for example, after dropping from 1.74 in 2012 to 1.49 in 2014, jumped to 2.11 in 2017. This means small builders could cover their immediate debts twice with the amount of current assets they hold.

In addition, the debt-to-equity ratio fell below 1 (to 0.75) in 2017, less than half what it was in 2012 (1.94) or 2014 (2.32). A lower debt-to-equity ratio means companies are less leveraged and rely less heavily on debt to run their

Table 5.3. Balance Sheet

	2012		2014		2017	
	Average ($1,000s)	Share of total (%)	Average ($1,000s)	Share of total (%)	Average ($1,000s)	Share of total (%)
Assets						
Current assets						
Cash	211	11.2	297	12.7	218	12.2
Receivables and inventories	n/a	n/a	n/a	n/a	358	20.0
Construction work in progress	1,010	53.7	1,195	50.9	613	34.2
Other current assets	504	26.8	469	20.0	107	6.0
Total current assets	1,725	91.7	1,961	83.6	1,296	72.3
Other assets	155	8.3	385	16.4	497	27.7
Total assets	**1,880**	**100.0**	**2,346**	**100.0**	**1,794**	**100.0**
Liabilities						
Current liabilities	441	23.5	616	26.3	392	21.8
Construction loans payable	550	29.3	699	29.8	224	12.5
Total current liabilities	992	52.8	1,315	56.1	615	34.3
Long-term loans payable	n/a	n/a	n/a	n/a	84	4.7
Other long-term liabilities	249	13.2	325	13.9	71	3.9
Total liabilities	**1,241**	**66.0**	**1,640**	**69.9**	**770**	**42.9**
Owner's equity	**640**	**34.0**	**706**	**30.1**	**1,024**	**57.1**
Total liabilities & owner's equity	**1,880**	**100.0**	**2,346**	**100.0**	**1,794**	**100.0**

businesses — and therefore have less inherent risk. ROA also showed improvement, going from 9.9% in 2014 to 14% in 2017, while ROE slipped back from 32.8% to 24.5%, due mostly to strong growth in these builders' invested capital (Table 5.4).

Table 5.4. Financial Ratios

	2012	2014	2017
Current ratio	1.74	1.49	2.11
Debt-to-equity ratio	1.94	2.32	0.75
Return on assets (%)	7.00	9.90	14.0
Return on equity (%)	20.60	32.80	24.5

Small-Volume Builders with Land Costs

Average total revenue among small-volume builders with land costs (those with 25 or fewer closings that only build spec or pre-sold homes on their own lots) continued to increase in 2017. After reaching a cycle low of $2.1 million in 2010, their revenue has been growing steadily: $2.9 million in 2012, $3.5 million in 2014, and finally to $4.0 million in 2017 (Table 5.5).

Higher revenue translated into higher costs of sales in 2017. Small builders with land costs spent $3.2 million (79.2% of revenue) on costs of sales, compared to $2.6 million in 2014 (76.4%). Most of the increase stemmed from higher land costs, which took up 19.7% of revenue, up from 16.0% in 2014. After accounting for all costs, this group posted a gross profit of $830,000, a gross margin of 20.8% — about three percentage points lower than in 2014 (23.6%), but five points higher than in 2012 (15.9%).

Small-volume builders with land costs managed to significantly reduce their operating expenses in 2017, perhaps driven by the need to make up for the increased cost of sales described above. All together, operating expenses took up 12.5% of revenue, compared to 15.1% in 2014. Even owner's compensation declined from $123,000 (3.6% of revenue) to $93,000 (2.3%) (Table 5.6). In the end, net profit averaged $330,000, a net profit margin of 8.3% — the second-highest these builders have seen since records began in 2002 (after 8.5% in 2014). Figure 5.2 summarizes the income statement for small-volume

Table 5.5. Small-Volume Builders With Land Costs: Gross Profit

	2012		2014		2017	
	Average ($1,000s)	Share of revenue (%)	Average ($1,000s)	Share of revenue (%)	Average ($1,000s)	Share of revenue (%)
Revenue	2,896	100.0	3,467	100.0	3,997	100.0
Cost of sales						
Land costs	411	14.2	553	16.0	788	19.7
Direct costs: single-family	1,776	61.3	1,844	53.2	2,076	51.9
Direct costs: multifamily, remodeling, light commercial/industrial	131	4.5	147	4.2	204	5.1
Indirect construction costs	106	3.7	95	2.7	99	2.5
Other costs	10	0.3	9	0.3	0	0.0
Total cost of sales	2,434	84.1	2,647	76.4	3,167	79.2
Gross Profit	462	15.9	820	23.6	830	20.8

builders with land costs for 2017 (Appendix V.4.).

No balance sheet data are available for small-volume builders with land costs because of insufficient responses. For the same reason, no results can be tabulated for small builders without land costs at all, and for small combination builders, only balance sheet aggregates can be reliably calculated.

Small-Volume Combination Builders

Small combination builders (those building 25 or fewer homes per year either on their own land or their customers' land) responding in

Table 5.6. Small-Volume Builders With Land Costs: Net Profit

	2012		2014		2017	
	Average ($1,000s)	Share of revenue (%)	Average ($1,000s)	Share of revenue (%)	Average ($1,000s)	Share of revenue (%)
Gross profit	462	15.9	820	23.6	830	20.8
Operating expenses						
Financing expenses	38	1.3	64	1.8	64	1.6
Sales & marketing expenses	120	4.1	168	4.8	175	4.4
General & administrative expenses	155	5.3	170	4.9	165	4.1
Depreciation	n/a	n/a	n/a	n/a	2	0.1
Owner's compensation	34	1.2	123	3.6	93	2.3
Total operating expenses	346	11.9	525	15.1	500	12.5
Net profit (loss)	116	4.0	295	8.5	330	8.3

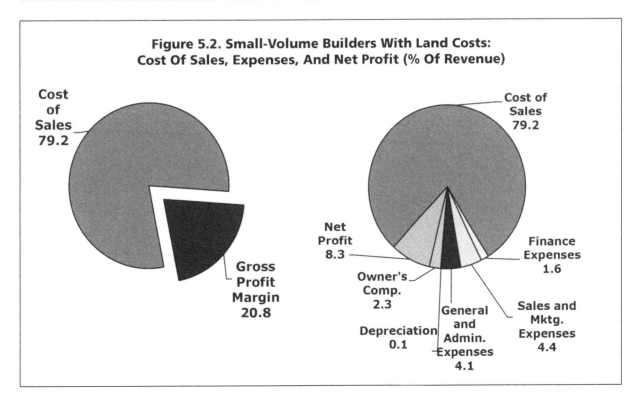

Figure 5.2. Small-Volume Builders With Land Costs: Cost Of Sales, Expenses, And Net Profit (% Of Revenue)

Cost of Sales 79.2

Gross Profit Margin 20.8

Cost of Sales 79.2

Net Profit 8.3

Owner's Comp. 2.3

Depreciation 0.1

General and Admin. Expenses 4.1

Sales and Mktg. Expenses 4.4

Finance Expenses 1.6

2017 were significantly smaller companies than similar types of builders responding to previous iterations of this study. Total assets, for example, averaged just $1.1 million, compared to $3.5 million in 2014 and $2.1 million in 2012 (Table 5.7). Small combination builders in 2017 reported substantially smaller amounts of both debt and invested capital: Total liabilities only reached $540,000 (compared to $2.4 million in 2014), while total equity averaged $576,000 (compared to $1.1 million in 2014) (Table 5.7).

Significantly reduced levels of debt led to improvements in some financial ratios. The current ratio rose to 1.98 (from 1.42 in 2014), while the debt-to-equity fell below 1 to 0.94 (from 2.28 in 2014) (Table 5.8). ROA and ROE cannot be calculated due to insufficient data to produce an average net profit margin for this group of builders.

Table 5.8. Small-volume Combination Builders: Financial Ratios

	2012	2014	2017
Current ratio	1.69	1.42	1.98
Debt-to-equity ratio	3.96	2.28	0.94

Table 5.7. Small-Volume Combination Builders: Balance Sheet

	2012		2014		2017	
	Average ($1,000s)	Share of total (%)	Average ($1,000s)	Share of total (%)	Average ($1,000s)	Share of total (%)
Assets						
Current assets						
Cash	184	8.8	362	10.5	264	23.6
Receivables and inventories	n/a	n/a	n/a	n/a	126	11.3
Construction work in progress	1,068	50.9	1,900	54.8	515	46.2
Other current assets	643	30.6	656	18.9	105	9.4
Total current assets	1,895	90.2	2,919	84.2	1,011	90.5
Other assets	205	9.8	546	15.8	106	9.5
Total assets	**2,100**	**100.0**	**3,465**	**100.0**	**1,116**	**100.0**
Liabilities						
Current liabilities	315	15.0	738	21.3	363	32.5
Construction loans payable	805	38.3	1,316	38.0	148	13.3
Total current liabilities	1,120	53.3	2,054	59.3	511	45.8
Long-term loans payable	n/a	n/a	n/a	n/a	22	2.0
Other long-term liabilities	557	26.5	356	10.3	7	0.6
Total liabilities	**1,677**	**79.9**	**2,410**	**69.5**	**540**	**48.4**
Owner's equity	423	20.1	1,055	30.5	576	51.6
Total liabilities & owner's equity	**2,100**	**100.0**	**3,465**	**100.0**	**1,116**	**100.0**

6

Production Builders

All Production Builders Combined

For the purpose of this study, a production builder is one that closes 26 or more units per year. According to the 2017 NAHB Builder Member Census, approximately 19% of our association's Builder members fall in this category. Total revenue for the typical production builder in 2017 was $29.8 million, about 4% lower than in 2014 ($31.1 million), and about the same level as in 2012 ($29.4 million). On average, these builders spent 81.2% of revenue ($24.2 million) on costs of sales, essentially the same share they spent in 2014 (81.0%). In the end, they finished 2017 with $5.6 million in gross profits, for an 18.8% gross margin — just slightly below the 19% reported in 2014 (Table 6.1).

In addition to maintaining a tight lid on costs of sales, production builders have also managed to consistently reduce how much of their revenue is spent on operating expenses. In 2008, that share was 18.9%, but was driven down to 15.7% in 2010, 12.9% in 2012, 12.2% in 2014, and then 11.4% in 2017 (the smallest share in the history of the series). After subtracting these expenses, production builders finished 2017 with $2.2 million in net profits, for a net margin of 7.5% — the highest seen by this group of builders since 2006 (8.4%) (Table 6.2). Figure 6.1 summarizes the income statement for production builders for 2017 (Appendix V.3).

Much like other types of builders, production builders also reported considerably smaller bal-

Table 6.1. Gross Profit

	2012		2014		2017	
	Average ($1,000s)	Share of revenue (%)	Average ($1,000s)	Share of revenue (%)	Average ($1,000s)	Share of revenue (%)
Revenue	29,361	100.0	31,089	100.0	29,766	100.0
Cost of sales						
Land costs	5,086	17.3	4,847	15.6	3,870	13.0
Direct costs: single-family	17,767	60.5	18,627	59.9	18,613	62.5
Direct costs: multifamily, remodeling, light commercial/industrial	118	0.4	396	1.3	744	2.5
Indirect construction costs	732	2.5	894	2.9	836	2.8
Other costs	384	1.3	431	1.4	95	0.3
Total cost of sales	24,087	82.0	25,195	81.0	24,158	81.2
Gross profit	**5,274**	**18.0**	**5,894**	**19.0**	**5,608**	**18.8**

Table 6.2. Net Profit

	2012		2014		2017	
	Average ($1,000s)	Share of revenue (%)	Average ($1,000s)	Share of revenue (%)	Average ($1,000s)	Share of revenue (%)
Gross profit	5,274	18.0	5,894	19.0	5,608	18.8
Operating expenses						
Financing expenses	534	1.8	518	1.7	398	1.3
Sales & mktg. expenses	1,650	5.6	1,667	5.4	1,479	5.0
General & administrative expenses	1,443	4.9	1,242	4.0	1,220	4.1
Depreciation	n/a	n/a	n/a	n/a	35	0.1
Owner's compensation	150	0.5	360	1.2	254	0.9
Total operating expenses	3,777	12.9	3,788	12.2	3,386	11.4
Net profit (loss)	1,496	5.1	2,106	6.8	2,221	7.5

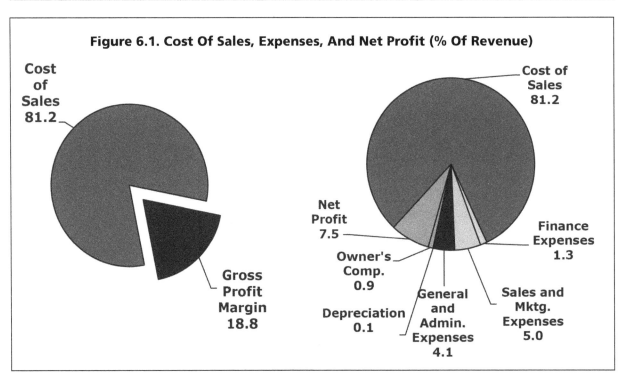

Figure 6.1. Cost Of Sales, Expenses, And Net Profit (% Of Revenue)

ance sheets in 2017 than in 2014. More specifically, their total assets averaged $14.5 million, about 27% lower than in 2014 ($19.9 million) and 21% lower than in 2012 ($18.2 million). The vast majority of their assets (92.0%) was in the form of current assets, with 72.2% of that held as construction work in progress. Current assets had made up more than 90% of all assets in 2012 and 2014 as well (Table 6.3).

The decline in assets was accompanied by drops in both total debt and equity. From 2014 to 2017, liabilities fell 24% from $13.6 million to $10.3 million, while equity fell 34% from $6.3 million to $4.1 million. As a result, the share of assets financed through debt rose from 68.5% in 2014 to 71.3% in 2017, while the share financed through owner's equity dropped from 31.5% to 28.7%.

Table 6.3. Balance Sheet

	2012		2014		2017	
	Average ($1,000s)	Share of total (%)	Average ($1,000s)	Share of total (%)	Average ($1,000s)	Share of total (%)
Assets						
Current assets						
Cash	1,234	6.8	1,178	5.9	924	6.4
Receivables and inventories	n/a	n/a	n/a	n/a	905	6.3
Construction work in progress	12,657	69.5	14,378	72.4	10,440	72.2
Other current assets	2,584	14.2	2,604	13.1	1,034	7.2
Total current assets	16,475	90.5	18,160	91.5	13,302	92.0
Other assets	1,724	9.5	1,690	8.5	1,151	8.0
Total assets	18,199	100.0	19,850	100.0	14,454	100.0
Liabilities						
Current liabilities	3,758	20.6	3,836	19.3	3,819	26.4
Construction loans payable	6,344	34.9	7,322	36.9	5,141	35.6
Total current liabilities	10,102	55.5	11,157	56.2	8,960	62.0
Long-term loans payable	n/a	n/a	n/a	n/a	1,305	9.0
Other long-term liabilities	1,550	8.5	2,433	12.3	43	0.3
Total liabilities	11,652	64.0	13,590	68.5	10,308	71.3
Owner's equity	6,548	36.0	6,260	31.5	4,146	28.7
Total liabilities & owner's equity	18,199	100.0	19,850	100.0	14,454	100.0

The financial ratios analyzed in this study show a mixed bag for production builders. In 2017, they earned 15.4% on assets and 53.6% on equity, improving their effectiveness at turning assets and equity into profits, from the 10.6% and 33.6% posted in 2014, respectively (Table 6.4). However, the current ratio declined slightly, from 1.63 to 1.48, and the debt-to-equity ratio rose from 2.17 to 2.49, showing increased reliance on debt to finance assets.

Table 6.4. Financial Ratios

	2012	2014	2017
Current ratio	1.63	1.63	1.48
Debt-to-equity ratio	1.78	2.17	2.49
Return on assets (%)	8.20	10.6	15.4
Return on equity (%)	22.90	33.6	53.6

No results can be tabulated for production builders without land costs because of insufficient responses, while for production combination builders, only balance sheet aggregates can be reliably calculated.

Production Combination Builders

After plunging from $23.2 million in 2008 to $11.1 million in 2010, average assets among production combination builders (those building 26 or more homes per year either on their own land or their customers' land) bounced back strongly in 2012 ($18.1 million) and 2014 ($18.4 million), before receding a bit in 2017 ($16.7 million) (Table 6.5). Current assets in 2017 made up 93% of all assets, most of which were held as construction work in progress (75.6%).

Table 6.5. Production Combination Builders: Balance Sheet

	2012		2014		2017	
	Average ($1,000s)	Share of total (%)	Average ($1,000s)	Share of total (%)	Average ($1,000s)	Share of total (%)
Assets						
Current assets						
Cash	969	5.4	944	5.1	694	4.2
Receivables and inventories	n/a	n/a	n/a	n/a	1,086	6.5
Construction work in progress	12,223	67.6	14,702	79.7	12,618	75.6
Other current assets	2,534	13.0	1,919	10.4	1,122	6.7
Total current assets	15,535	86.0	17,566	95.3	15,521	93.0
Other assets	2,534	14.0	876	4.7	1,160	7.0
Total assets	18,069	100.0	18,442	100.0	16,681	100.0
Liabilities						
Current liabilities	3,218	17.8	2,868	15.5	6,006	36.0
Construction loans payable	5,917	32.7	6,832	37.0	4,907	29.4
Total current liabilities	9,135	50.6	9,699	52.6	10,913	65.4
Long-term loans payable	n/a	n/a	n/a	n/a	1,081	6.5
Other long-term liabilities	2,473	13.7	896	4.9	77	0.5
Total liabilities	11,608	64.2	10,595	57.5	12,070	72.4
Owner's equity	6,461	35.8	7,847	42.5	4,610	27.6
Total liabilities & owner's equity	18,069	100.0	18,442	100.0	16,681	100.0

On the other side of the ledger, production combination builders showed $10.9 million in current liabilities and another $1.2 million in long-term liabilities, for a total of $12.1 million in combined debt. In 2014, in comparison, their total debt averaged $10.6 million. As a result, 72.4% of all assets held by this group of builders in 2017 was backed by debt, compared to a much lower 57.5% in 2014. Meanwhile, their average invested capital fell to $4.6 million in 2017 (from $7.8 million in 2014), lowering the equity share of assets to 27.6% (from 42.5%).

Higher levels of debt caused deterioration in some financial ratios for production combination builders. The combined effect of lower current assets and higher current liabilities led the current ratio to drop to 1.42 in 2017, from 1.81 in 2014 (and 1.70 in 2012). Similarly, the near duplication of the debt-to-equity ratio, from 1.35 to 2.62, shows much higher levels of leverage (and risk) in 2017 than in 2014 (Table 6.6).

Table 6.6. Production Combination Builders: Financial Ratios

	2012	2014	2017
Current ratio	1.70	1.81	1.42
Debt-to-equity ratio	1.80	1.35	2.62

7

Builder Financial Performance by Region and Business Model

The vast majority of revenue earned in 2017 by builders responding to *The Cost of Doing Business Study* survey (95.5%) originated from the construction of single-family homes. Each of the other activities brought in less than 2% of revenue: multifamily home building (1.9%), residential remodeling (1.0%), light commercial (0.4%), and all other sources combined (1.2%).

Revenue and Profits by Region

Builders in both the Midwest and South reported that exactly 97.2% of all their 2017 revenue was derived from single-family home building. In the West region, that share was smaller at 91.1%.

This revenue source breakdown cannot be produced for the Northeast because insufficient responses for this region make any estimates statistically unreliable.

As is typically the case, builders in the Midwest spent a relatively smaller share of revenue on land (4.4%) than their counterparts in the South (15.6%) or West (14.9%). But as is also usual, Midwestern builders spent a significantly larger proportion of revenue on direct construction costs (e.g. labor and materials) for single-family home building (73.2%) than builders in the South (62.1%) or in the West (55.1%) (Figure 7.1). In the end, builders in the Midwest posted a gross profit margin of

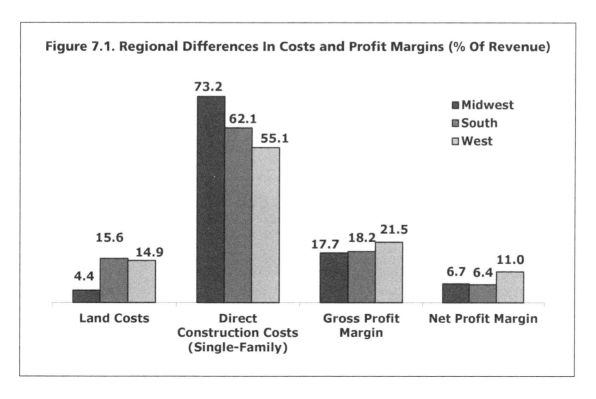

Figure 7.1. Regional Differences In Costs and Profit Margins (% Of Revenue)

- Midwest
- South
- West

Land Costs: 4.4, 15.6, 14.9
Direct Construction Costs (Single-Family): 73.2, 62.1, 55.1
Gross Profit Margin: 17.7, 18.2, 21.5
Net Profit Margin: 6.7, 6.4, 11.0

17.7%, compared to 18.2% among builders in the South and 21.5% among those in the West.

On average, builders in the South spent 11.7% on operating expenses, slightly more than builders in the Midwest (11.0%) and West (10.4%). The most important of these expenses in the Midwest and South was sales and marketing expenses, which accounted for 5.1% of revenue in both regions. In the West, the largest share was paid for general and administrative expenses, which took up 4.2%. After subtracting these various expenses from gross profits, builders in the West reported the highest net profit margin of all three regions, at 11.0%, compared with 6.7% in the Midwest and 6.4% in the South.

Builders in the South and West regions continued to see improvements in their bottom lines in 2017, as their net margins exceeded those posted in 2014 (6.1% and 6.8%, respectively), which in turn had exceeded those for 2012 (3.5% and 5.2%, respectively). The net profit margin for builders in the Midwest, meanwhile, had improved in recent years, from 0.9% in 2010 to 5.2% in 2012 and 7.3% in 2014, but receded slightly in 2017 to 6.7%.

Revenue and Profits by Business Model

In 2008, for the first time in the history of *The Cost of Doing Business Study,* builders without land costs posted a higher net profit margin (5.1%) than either combination builders (-2.5%) or those with land costs (-4.9%). The same was true in 2010. But in 2012, builders with land costs regained the top spot, with an average net margin of 6.2%, compared with 3.6% for combination builders and 4.2% for those without land costs. In 2014, the title of most profitable group went to combination builders, with a net margin of 7.6% vs. 5.9% for builders with land costs and 3.6% for those without land costs.

In 2017, the top spot switched back to builders with land costs, which posted an impressive average net profit margin of 10.3% (Figure 7.2). With revenue averaging $14.7 million, these builders reported the strongest gross profit margin (20.9%) of the three business models analyzed, and only paid their owners 1% of revenue in compensation.

Meanwhile, combination builders earned an average of $19.9 million in 2017, spent 82.8%

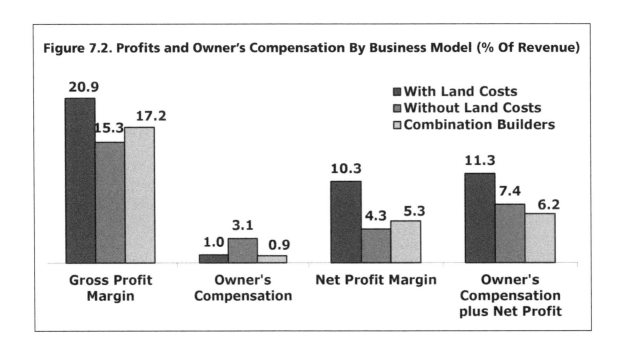

Figure 7.2. Profits and Owner's Compensation By Business Model (% Of Revenue)

■ With Land Costs
■ Without Land Costs
□ Combination Builders

Gross Profit Margin: 20.9, 15.3, 17.2
Owner's Compensation: 1.0, 3.1, 0.9
Net Profit Margin: 10.3, 4.3, 5.3
Owner's Compensation plus Net Profit: 11.3, 7.4, 6.2

on costs of sales (67% of that on direct construction costs for single-family homes), and therefore posted a 17.2% gross profit margin. Another 11.9% of their revenue went to pay for operating expenses, the highest of which was sales and marketing expenses (5.2%) and the lowest depreciation (0.1%), leaving them with a net profit margin of 5.3%.

Builders without land costs had much lower revenue — $6.1 million on average, but the highest relative costs of sales (84.7%) of all three business models, which led them to have the lowest gross margin (15.3%). They spent 11.1% of revenue on operating expenses, including 3.1% on owner's compensation, leaving them with a net profit margin of 4.3% — the lowest of the three business models.

Although comparing net profit margins across business models is useful, it may not tell the complete story on profitability. A more comprehensive way to look at builders' overall performance is to add the company's net profit margin to the share spent on owner's compensation, because there may be little distinction between the two line items, especially, in small companies.

According to this broader measure of profitability for 2017, builders with land costs had better performance (11.3%) than builders without land costs (7.4%), or production builders (6.2%). In 2014, this comprehensive measure was smaller for builders with land costs (7.4%) and for those without land costs (6.5%), but a bit larger for combination builders (8.8%).

Not only did builders with land cost have the highest profit margins in 2017, they also had the largest balance sheets, with an average of $8.6 million in total assets (Figure 7.3). Of that amount, $5.3 million was held as construction work in progress and only $686,000 in cash. Current and long term-liabilities averaged $5.6 million (64.4% of all assets), while owner's equity averaged $3.1 million (35.6% of assets).

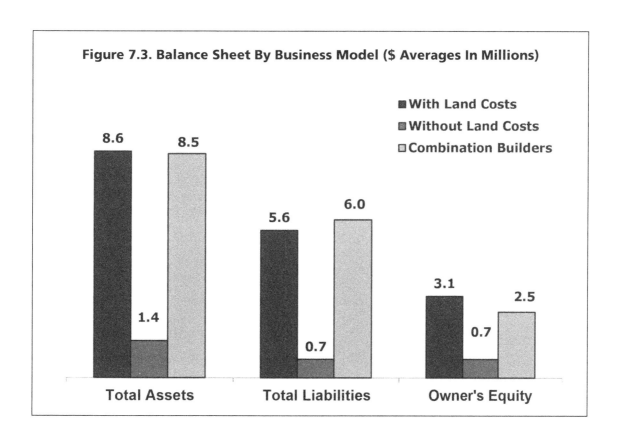

Figure 7.3. Balance Sheet By Business Model ($ Averages In Millions)

- With Land Costs
- Without Land Costs
- Combination Builders

	Total Assets	Total Liabilities	Owner's Equity
With Land Costs	8.6	5.6	3.1
Without Land Costs	1.4	0.7	0.7
Combination Builders	8.5	6.0	2.5

Combination builders had the second highest level of assets, averaging $8.5 million. Of that amount, $6.3 million was tied to construction work in progress and only $469,000 was cash. Their average liabilities were $6.0 million (70.7% of assets) and their average equity $2.5 million (29.3% of assets).

Of the three business models, builders without land costs had the lowest average assets at $1.4 million. About $307,000 was cash, $441,000 was in receivables and inventories, and another $432,000 in construction work in progress. This group of builders reported an average of $668,000 (49.4% of assets) in total liabilities and $685,000 in equity (50.6% of assets).

8

Operations

The vast majority — 86% — of respondents to this *The Cost of Doing Business Study* indicated their primary activity was single-family home building. More specifically, 38% reported to be single-family production builders, 30% single-family custom builders — on the owner's lot, and another 18% single-family custom builders — on the builder's lots (Figure 8.1). Another 7% of respondents were primarily residential remodelers, 2% were land developers, and 1% each multifamily builders for-rent and multi-family condominium builders. As stated previously, only respondents whose primary opera-

tion was single-family home building were included in the financial analysis presented throughout this report.

Number of Years in Business

Respondents to *The Cost of Doing Business Study* have been in business for an average of 23 years. Less than a quarter (23%) have been in the residential construction industry for 10 years or less, 21% for 11 to 19 years, 25% for 20 to 29 years, and the remaining 31% for 30 years or longer (Figure 8.2).

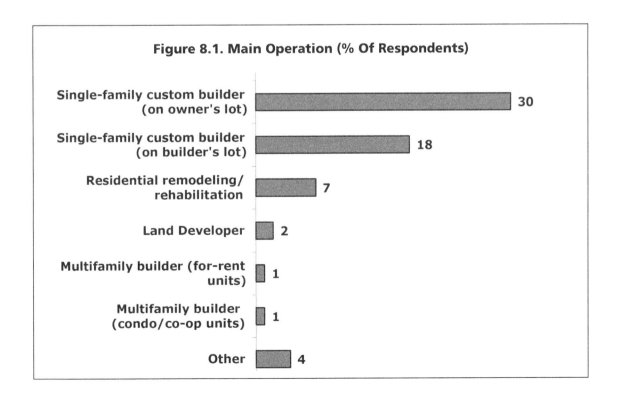

Figure 8.1. Main Operation (% Of Respondents)

Operation	%
Single-family custom builder (on owner's lot)	30
Single-family custom builder (on builder's lot)	18
Residential remodeling/rehabilitation	7
Land Developer	2
Multifamily builder (for-rent units)	1
Multifamily builder (condo/co-op units)	1
Other	4

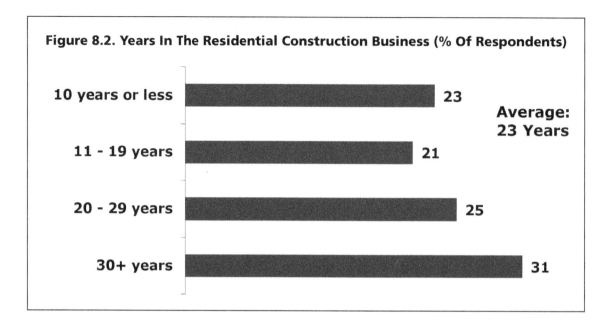

Figure 8.2. Years In The Residential Construction Business (% Of Respondents)

10 years or less	23
11 - 19 years	21
20 - 29 years	25
30+ years	31

Average: 23 Years

Results show a direct positive relationship between years in business and the amount of revenue builders earned in 2017. Among those with less than $2 million in revenue, for example, average tenure in the industry was 22 years, compared to an average of 23 years among those earning $2 million to $9.9 million, and 25 years among those with revenue of $10 million or more (Appendix V.1).

Looking at tenure across business models shows that builders with land costs have been in the industry the longest — an average of 29 years. Combination builders come in second with an average of 21 years in residential construction, followed by builders without land costs, with an average tenure of 19 years. Across regions of the country, builders in the Midwest have been in the industry the longest — an average of 31 years, compared to 23 years for those in the West and 20 years for builders in the South.

Units Closed: Presold, Speculative, or on Customers' Land

Respondents to *The Cost of Doing Business Study* closed an average of 38 units in 2017. Of those,

16 (43%) were pre-sold on the builders' lots, 12 (31%) were built speculatively (without a buyer at the time of start), and 10 (26%) were built directly on the owner's land (Figure 8.3). Their average number of closings in 2017 was smaller than in 2006 (52 units), better than in 2008 or 2010 (24 units both years), but lower than in 2012 (46 units) or 2014 (42 units). Census data on the purpose of construction show that 80% of all single-family units started in 2017 were built for sale (either pre-sold or spec), 14% were built on the owner's land by a contractor, and 7% were built directly by the owner.

Builders with land costs closed an average of 39 single-family homes in 2017 (25 pre-sold, 14 speculative), a significant reduction from the 64 homes reported by this type of builder in 2014. Given the 31% increase in overall single-family production nationwide between 2014 and 2017 (from 648,000 to 849,000 units started), this decline is likely the result of a shift in the mix of builders responding to the survey in 2017 rather than an actual decline in the levels of production among builders with land costs during this period.

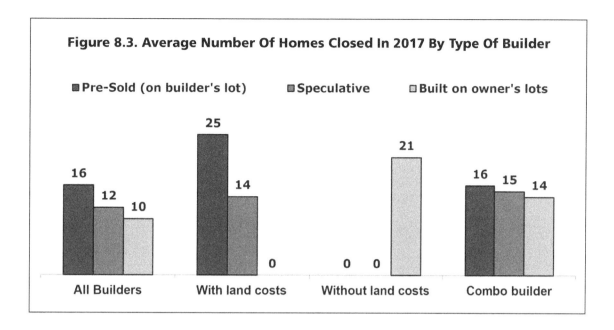

Figure 8.3. Average Number Of Homes Closed In 2017 By Type Of Builder

Builders without land costs closed an average of 21 homes on land owned by their customers, a significant jump from the 13 homes this type of builder reported closing in both 2012 and 2014. This increase is also likely the result of a change in the mix of builders without land costs responding in 2017, as the share of all single-family starts built by contractors (on the owner's land) fell from 17% in 2014 to 14% in 2017.

Combination builders, meanwhile, closed on 45 homes in 2017, slightly ahead of the 41 units this group reported in 2014, but still below the 57 homes they reported closing on in 2012. Of the 45 closings, 16 were pre=sold, 15 speculative, and 14 were built on the owner's land.

9

Historical Data and Trends

The analysis of single-family builders' financial statements for 2017 shows these companies remain on a path of gradual and steady recovery following the housing recession of the late 2000s. In 2008, builders reported the worst financial performance in the history of this series, with a net profit margin of -3%. In 2010, they barely broke even, with a net margin of 0.5%. Yet in 2012, they returned to healthier profit levels (4.9%), followed by slow but steady gains in 2014 (6.4%) and 2017 (7.6%). Historically, these last two readings on net profitability are higher than the average reported in all *The Cost of Doing Business Studies* between 1985 and 2017, 5.3% (Table 9.1).

Table 9.1. Summary Data From The NAHB Cost Of Doing Business Studies (% Of Revenue)

	Total Sales	Cost of Sales	Gross Profit	Operating Expenses Breakdown					Total Operating Expense	Net Income Before Tax
				Finance	Sales and Marketing	General & Administrative	Depreciation	Owner's Compensation		
2017	100.0%	81.0%	19.0%	1.3%	4.7%	4.1%	0.1%	1.2%	11.4%	7.6%
2014	100	81.1	18.9	1.4	5	4.7		1.3	12.5	6.4
2012	100	82.6	17.4	1.7	5.1	5		0.8	12.5	4.9
2010	100	84.7	15.3	2.1	5.2	5.8		1.6	14.7	0.5
2008	100	85.6	14.4	2.8	5.4	7.5		1.7	17.4	-3
2006	100	79.2	20.8	2.5	4.4	5		1.3	13.1	7.7
2004	100	79.1	20.9	1.5	4.7	5.4		1.3	12.9	8
2002	100	81.1	18.9	0.6	2.6	5.9		4.5	13.6	5.4
2000	100	80.1	19.9	2.2	5.7	3.9		1.8	13.5	6.3
1996	100	82.4	17.6	1.5	3.3	5		3.4	13.2	4.4
1993	100	79.4	20.6	1.9	4	5.1		5	16	4.6
1991	100	78	22	3	4	5			12	10
1989	100	79.1	20.9	5.6	5.2	4.8			15.6	5.3
1987	100	79.7	20.3	3.3	3.7	6.1			13.1	7.2
1985	100	81.7	18.3	3.9	3.3	7.6			14.8	3.5
1983*	100	79.7	20.3	4.5	3.3	8.8			17.6	2.7
1980*	100	77.2	22.8	2	2.5	9.4			16.9	5.9
1978	100	76.1	23.9	2.7	3.6	5.5			16.9	7
1975	100	84.1	15.9	2.8	2.3	7.5			11.6	4.3
1970	100	82.4	17.6	3.3	3	6.5			14.4	3.2

* The Values for 1980 and 1983 are medians.

Note: The years in this table represent the years the data was collected for, not the years in the book titles.

Source: NAHB

In terms of their share of builders' revenue, costs of sales (land, direct, and indirect construction costs) averaged about 80% from 1985 until 2006, before skyrocketing to 85.6% after the housing recession in 2008. Costs of sales have fallen every year since then, but still averaged about 83% in the decade from 2008 to 2017. There was essentially no change in this share from 2014 (81.1%) to 2017 (81.0%).

Given these trends in costs, builders' average gross margins also saw an inflection point after 2006. In fact, from 1985 until 2006, their average gross margin stood at 20%. In 2008, it fell to 14.4%, which is part of the reason why the average from 2008 to 2017 is "only" 17%. There was essentially no change in builders' gross margins from 2014 (18.9%) to 2017 (19.0%).

Operating expenses were also greatly impacted by the housing recession. In 2006, they accounted for 13.1% of all revenue, before jumping to 17.4% in 2008. In the years since, however, builders have been successful at bringing them down: to 14.7% in 2010, 12.5% in both 2012 and 2014, and then to 11.4% in 2017. An interesting fact is that average operating expenses represented 13.8% of builders' revenue from 1985 until 2006, essentially the same share as from 2008 to 2017, 13.7%.

Construction Cost Surveys

In addition to *The Cost of Doing Business Study* surveys, NAHB periodically conducts a construction cost survey asking builders to break down costs and expenses of their typical homes as follows: finished lot cost, construction costs, financing costs, overhead and general expenses, marketing costs, sales commissions,

and profits. The data are national averages because the sample size does not allow for regional breakdowns. Although they are not a perfect tool for estimating the costs of a particular house, the results can provide a broad idea of construction costs for a typical home. Table 9.2 summarizes the results through 2017, the last time NAHB conducted the survey. A complete article on the findings is available at nahb.org/2017constructioncosts.

According to the 2017 results, about 21.5% of a typical home's sales price pays for the finished lot, which includes raw land and development costs. Construction costs (labor, materials, and subcontractors) account for more than half the price of a home: 55.6%, while overhead and general expenses take up 5.1%, sales commissions 4.1%, financing costs 1.8%, marketing costs 1.2%, and finally, pre-tax profit 10.7%.

When reading the data in tables 9.1 and 9.2, it is important to keep in mind that results from *The Cost of Doing Business Study* (Table 9.1) are based on company-wide operations, so the percentages are of total revenue spent on expenses from all operations combined. Data from the construction cost survey (Table 9.2), on the other hand, are based on builders' estimates of how the price of an individual home is allocated among various categories, so the numbers there represent percentages of an average home's price, not of total company revenue. It is also important to mention that the results shown in Table 9.2 are based on surveys that do not control for the characteristics of the homes sampled, and so the data on prices, square footage, and lot size may change from one survey to the next in ways that do not reflect overall national trends.

Table 9.2. Cost Breakdown Of Single-Family Home (% Of Sales Price)

	1995	1998	2002	2004	2007	2009	2011	2013	2015	2017
Finished Lot Cost	24.4	23.6	23.5	26.0	24.5	20.3	21.7	18.6	18.2	21.5
Total Construction Cost	53.3	54.8	50.8	51.7	48.1	58.9	59.3	61.7	61.8	55.6
Financing Cost	2.0	1.9	2.1	1.8	2.4	1.7	2.1	1.4	1.3	1.8
Overhead & General Expenses	5.8	5.7	5.5	5.8	7.0	5.4	5.2	4.3	5.6	5.1
Marketing Cost	2.2	1.4	2.4	1.9	2.5	1.4	1.5	1.1	0.8	1.2
Sales Commission	3.3	3.4	3.7	3.0	4.3	3.4	3.3	3.6	3.2	4.1
Profit	9.1	9.2	12.0	9.8	11.2	8.9	6.8	9.3	9.0	10.7
Total	**100.0**	**100.0**	**100.0**	**100.0**	**100.0**	**100.0**	**100.0**	**100.0**	**100.0**	**100.0**
Sales Price	**$183,585**	**$226,680**	**$298,412**	**$373,349**	**$454,906**	**$377,624**	**$310,619**	**$399,532**	**$468,318**	**$427,892**

Source: NAHB Surveys of Builder Members
Note: 2002 data based on survey of Builder members carried out in late 2002-early 2003.

Public Firms

The financial reports of publicly traded home building companies offer another view of profitability in the construction industry. Table 9.3 shows revenue, as well as pretax and post-tax profits, for 13 public builders from 2015 to 2017[1]. When aggregated, they earned total revenue of $66.9 billion in 2017, essentially the same as in 2016 ($66.2 billion), but 24% more than in 2015 ($54.1 billion), and three times more than in 2011 ($22.1 billion)! Despite the improvement in recent years, however, aggregate revenue among public builders is still significantly below the $106.8 billion they posted in 2006.

All but one of the public builders in Table 9.3 posted positive pretax profits for fiscal year 2017. Hovnanian Enterprises, the sole exception, had pretax losses in the amount of $45 million. Altogether, this group's pretax profits reached $7.4 billion, about the same as in 2016

($7.3 billion), but 22% higher than in 2015 ($6.1 billion). After paying for corporate taxes in 2017, their profit was $3.7 billion (including a $332 million after-tax loss by Hovnanian), 11% lower than in 2016 ($4.2 billion), and back to the same level as in 2015 ($3.7 billion)

Under pre-2018 tax law, all businesses could claim operating losses from previous tax years as a deduction against current year net income, thereby reducing current year tax liability. Losses could be carried forward for up to 20 years. Such claims acted to increase after-tax income for accounting purposes by realizing a previously deferred tax asset as income. In other words, the deferred asset, which had potential future value as a future tax deduction, increased after-tax income when realized. The tax deduction reduced taxable income in the year to which it was carried forward, thus increasing after-tax income by reducing taxes paid. The last time this group of public builders' after-tax profits were higher than before filing with the IRS was in 2013, when they averaged $5.3 billion, compared to $4.1 billion prior to filing.

---

[1] Data provided are for each builder's fiscal year, which does not necessarily correspond to the calendar year.

Table 9.3. Publicly Traded Builders ($ Millions)

	2015			2016			2017		
	Revenue	Pretax Profit	After-tax Profit	Revenue	Pretax Profit	After-tax Profit	Revenue	Pretax Profit	After-tax Profit
D.R. Horton	10,824	1,123	751	12,157	1,354	886	14,091	1,602	1,038
Lennar	9,474	1,210	803	10,950	1,330	912	12,646	1,190	810
Pulte Group	5,841	757	494	7,487	861	603	8,381	865	447
CalAtlantic*	3,540	342	214	6,477	753	485	--	--	--
NVR	5,065	555	383	5,709	601	425	6,176	776	538
Toll Brothers	4,171	536	363	5,170	589	382	5,815	814	535
Taylor Morrison	2,977	568	61	3,550	680	53	3,885	739	91
KB Homes	3,032	127	85	3,595	149	106	4,369	290	181
Meritage Homes	2,079	189	129	2,498	218	150	2,660	248	143
MDC Holdings	1,909	101	66	2,327	152	103	2,578	230	142
Hovnanian Enterprises	2,148	22	(16)	2,752	2	(3)	2,452	(45)	(332)
Beazer	1,627	272	344	1,822	297	5	1,916	313	32
M/I	1,418	300	52	1,691	329	57	1,962	393	72
Total	**54,105**	**6,102**	**3,729**	**66,185**	**7,315**	**4,164**	**66,931**	**7,415**	**3,697**

*CalAtlantic was acquired by Lennar in 2018.

The Tax Cuts and Jobs Act (TCJA) passed at the end of 2017, however, placed limits on the use of net operating losses so that, starting in tax year 2018, businesses may no longer use them to offset all of their taxable income in subsequent years. In oversimplified terms, the deduction is now limited to 80% of a business' taxable income and it must be applied in the first tax year in which it has positive taxable income, but may also be carried indefinitely, rather than limited to a 20-year period. For a more thorough understanding of the impact of the TCJA on businesses, visit NAHB Economics Group's blog (EyeOnHousing.org) and review the Tax Reform Toolkit.

Actual annual pre-tax profit margins for each of the 13 public builders are shown in Table 9.4 going back more than a decade. These data show that this group's combined average pre-tax margin has remained close to 11% every year since 2013, narrowly fluctuating from 10.8% in 2013 to 11.6% in 2014 and staying in that range in 2017, at 11.3%. Looking back, this group experienced dramatic losses during the housing recession, posting negative pre-tax margins every year from 2007 to 2011, with the worst loss occurring in 2008, at -29.4%. Prior to the recession, from 2002 to 2006, these builders' aggregate margins averaged 12.7%.

Table 9.4. Pretax Profit Margins For Publicly Traded Builders (%)

	2002	2003	2004	2005	2006	2007	2008	2009	2010	2011	2012	2013	2014	2015	2016	2017
D.R. Horton	9.6	11.5	14.6	16.7	12.7	-9.2	-40.9	-15.0	2.3	0.3	5.7	10.5	10.1	10.4	11.1	11.4
Lennar	12.1	13.5	14.5	16.2	6.0	-31.7	-13.2	-26.8	3.1	3.2	5.4	11.5	12.5	12.8	12.1	9.4
Pulte	9.8	11.1	13.7	15.4	7.2	-27.5	-27.7	-46.7	-27.0	-7.5	3.8	8.6	11.1	13.0	11.5	10.3
CalAtlantic	--	--	--	--	--	--	--	--	--	--	--	--	--	9.7	11.6	--
NVR	17.1	18.9	20.1	22.1	16.0	10.7	4.6	11.1	10.8	8.0	8.8	9.2	9.8	11.0	10.5	12.6
Toll Brothers	14.9	14.8	16.6	22.8	18.4	1.6	-14.8	-28.3	-7.8	-2.0	6.0	10.0	12.9	12.9	11.4	14.0
Taylor Morrison*	--	--	--	--	--	--	--	--	--	--	--	21.7	20.9	19.1	19.2	19.0
Ryland**	10.7	11.5	13.2	15.0	11.9	-13.8	-20.5	-20.2	-8.0	-3.7	3.4	9.2	10.9	--	--	--
Standard Pacific**	10.3	14.2	15.3	17.7	6.1	-29.0	-79.6	-9.2	-1.3	-1.8	6.2	13.3	14.4	--	--	--
KB Homes	9.3	9.5	10.2	13.7	6.1	-22.8	-31.9	-12.7	-4.8	-13.8	-5.1	1.8	4.0	4.2	4.1	6.6
Meritage Homes	10.2	10.3	11.0	13.9	10.5	-19.5	-18.1	-16.0	0.2	-2.3	2.4	9.8	9.6	9.0	8.7	9.3
MDC Holdings	11.8	11.9	15.9	16.9	7.2	-27.3	-28.1	-11.9	-7.4	-12.7	5.1	7.7	5.9	5.3	6.5	8.9
Hovnanian Enterprises	8.9	12.9	13.2	14.6	3.8	-13.5	-35.3	-42.1	-21.5	-25.7	-6.8	1.2	1.0	1.0	0.1	-1.8
Beazer	7.6	9.0	9.9	10.0	10.8	-18.2	-41.8	-18.9	8.4	6.5	10.4	16.6	18.0	16.7	16.3	16.3
M/I	--	--	--	--	--	-14.8	-35.4	-16.3	-4.4	-6.0	19.4	19.9	20.8	21.2	19.5	20.0
Average	11.0	12.4	14.0	16.2	9.7	-16.5	-29.4	-19.5	-4.4	-4.4	5.0	10.8	11.6	11.3	11.0	11.3

*Taylor Morrison became a public company in 2013.

**Ryland and Standard Pacific merged to form CalAtlantic in 2015.

Developing Cost Control Systems

Bob Whitten

Successful builders know that controlling costs is the single most effective way to ensure profitability — and those same builders know that profitability is the single best measure of overall success. They understand how saving $100 on construction costs can yield more than $100 in higher profits. They understand that there is a synergy within operations when they learn to control cost. And they understand that when times get tough, cost control may be the *only* way to earn a profit.

Controlling costs accomplishes two things, both of which are critical to home building business success: It saves you money and it makes you money.

Let's take a look at how good cost control can impact builder profitability.

In this *Cost of Doing Business Study*, the "average" builder reported that 81% of each sales dollar goes to cover construction and land costs. That leaves 19% gross profit. Those figures have held relatively steady for a number of years.

Why Bother with a Cost Control System?

But who is content to be merely average? The top 25% of builders with land costs surveyed for this study had gross profit margins of 22.1%. This is over three points higher than the average. This is often the difference between a mediocre and an excellent year.

These results are still not where we set gross profit margin goals for the top-tier builders, where we are looking for 25+% in gross profit margin from home building operations.

A trend emerged when NAHB studied these top builders: Instead of simply accepting any financial results at the end of a project, top builders actively strive to control their costs. They have developed procedures, skills, and techniques to stay in control of their operations.

Ingredients of a Successful Cost-Control System

The following basic terms will help you understand why cost control has such a significant impact on profitability and why you need to implement a cost-control system for your business.

- **Cost-control system:** a set of procedures, activities, and techniques used to secure maximum gross profit from a job.
- **Gross profit:** the sum of sales price minus the construction cost. Gross profit is measured before operating expenses affect the profit picture.
- **Construction cost:** the "sticks and bricks" (materials) and the labor (either subcontracted or in house) associated with completing the construction phase of a project. For residential builders, cost of goods sold often include the cost of the finished lot the house occupies.

An effective cost-control system relies on a number of tools, which might include flow charts, monitoring reports, and critical area checklists. Building a successful system requires lots of planning, a little trial and error, and constant monitoring and followup.

The best cost-control systems actually integrate a number of subsystems, which typically correspond to the following key operational areas:

1. Product design and engineering
2. Construction planning
3. Estimating and purchasing
4. Construction quality control
5. Materials handling
6. Job cost accounting
7. Post-construction review and system improvement

This is certainly not an all-inclusive list, but it is an excellent starting point. As you can see, cost-control subsystems generally relate to each other in the same order as tasks in the general construction sequence. When all the subsystems work properly and operate together, builders can achieve remarkable success.

Because each home building business and each construction project can be different, it's difficult to estimate exactly how much you will save by reading this brief introduction to cost control and taking the advice. But I will cover the highlights of each component to demonstrate the detail involved.

Product Design and Engineering

When designing a new product, make sure you consider its cost-to-benefit ratio. A good rule of thumb is the more intricate the design, the less stable the costs and profit. By standardizing your plans and specifications as much as possible, you can gain control over your construction costs.

Whatever the design, use a detailed set of drawings reduced to 11 x 17" paper (wherever practical). Use these drawings to instruct each trade contractor on how to handle his or her part of the construction process in the most cost-effective way. Trades are a valuable source of ideas on how to improve the cost-effectiveness of your designs. Are you using them as part of your cost-control team?

Standardize as Much as Possible

Even custom home builders can benefit from design standards. Bathroom and kitchen modules can be designed to work in any home large enough to accommodate them. The same holds true for laundry rooms, home offices, media rooms, or just about any other recurring design element.

Designs based on standard engineering elements such as floor and roof trusses will keep the construction standards in place even in custom and semi-custom structures. Builders who use construction notebooks with detailed layout drawings showing proper drywall or sheathing patterns can reduce usage of these materials by two to three sheets in a 2,000-square-foot house. Developing these types of notebooks allows you to reduce waste and control costs. This same concept holds true in remodeling projects.

Some 'Standard' Specs Kill Profits

Watch out for "standard" amenities that should be buyer selections/options or allowances. Those costs can quickly eat into profits. Many builders include features in their standard specifications that really do not add value from the buyer's perspective. These specs are not structural elements of quality, nor are they essential to the buyer's purchasing decision or ultimate satisfaction. Instead, they usually reflect the builder's personal preferences, and only in his or her mind do they emerge as essential product ingredients.

Here's a classic example: One builder I know routinely includes insulation in all bathroom walls, both interior and exterior. He and his insulation crew are virtually the only people who know about this "value-added" feature. The sales staff certainly doesn't sell it as a benefit—they either don't realize the specification is included or they have grown so accustomed to it that they don't point it out anymore. The result? Most buyers don't even know that the bathrooms in their new homes are among the best insulated in the world!

The builder actually does himself a disservice in two ways: He spends money on a non-value-added, non-essential feature, and the buying public doesn't give him credit for being a better builder.

Contrast that with a builder who offers this same feature as an option. The sales staff receives training in how to sell the feature as an upgrade. Buyers feel like they have a choice. And when they buy the option, they feel good about their decision to do business with such an accommodating and service-minded builder. Finally, and most importantly, the builder covers the associated costs with the price of the upgrade and still can offer a more competitive base home price.

Pre-construction Planning

Setting specifications and construction schedules, negotiating with trades and suppliers, or producing purchase orders from pre-approved trade pricing agreements and training construction supervisors on the nuances of each new home are all part of preconstruction planning. Pre-construction planning gives you the opportunity to build the house many times on paper before the construction begins. You learn where problems may arise before the first shovel hits the dirt. That lets you identify mistakes before they occur, allowing you to take action to prevent problems and gain control during the construction process. Being in control from the start is far less expensive than costly crisis management.

Your construction planning process should include pre-construction meetings with buyers, trade contractors, employees, suppliers, and perhaps inspectors. Pre-construction meetings with buyers help eliminate change orders during construction and help establish mutual expectation levels. Communication improves when builders and buyers understand what the other expects, and everyone feels more in control during the construction process. A buyer who is satisfied during construction is easier and less stressful to work with.

Estimating, Purchasing, and Job Cost Accounting

Estimating, purchasing, and job cost accounting are the heart of most cost-control systems. They need to be very well integrated with each other.

Estimating

The more you know about your costs upfront, the better you can control them. Most successful builders base their estimates on a quantity takeoff method. That is, they calculate as carefully as possible the exact amount of every kind of material, supplies, equipment, and labor necessary to complete the construction project. That requires comprehensive, accurate, and up-to-date information on material and labor costs. For all companies, computerizing the estimating and takeoff information in a database will greatly improve the accuracy of bids, help control costs, and therefore increase profitability.

Purchasing

Home builders who build more than a few units a year have found that integrating their estimating and job cost accounting systems and using purchase orders (POs) has a tremendous impact on gross profits. POs ensure that there is a record of every purchase from the very start, well before materials are paid for or even delivered. PO systems prevent duplicate payments and ensure that what you originally estimated and ordered actually gets delivered to the jobsite. Furthermore, POs link every expenditure to a particular job, enabling builders to tie specific expenses to specific sources of revenue. That kind of information can significantly impact profitability significantly. In fact, builders have found that just using POs can add 5% or more to their gross profits.

Your purchasing system should include upfront price guarantees from trade contractors. By negotiating prices to cover a specific number of units or a certain period of time, you can plan more easily how your organization operates— and plan on higher profitability.

You should comparison shop to make sure your current vendors and labor sources offer competitive prices. Do this not to squeeze trade contractors or suppliers into making unreasonable concessions, but to ensure that you are not paying more than market prices or settling for inefficient services.

If you are a relatively large small-volume builder — handling perhaps 20 or 25 jobs per year — consider forming a purchasing committee to review your relationships with trade contractors and suppliers. A purchasing committee might include employees from your estimating, construction, sales, and operations departments. I know one very successful builder whose committee meets monthly. Whenever a vendor raises prices by 5% or more, the committee solicits three competitive bids and reviews the validity of the price increase. At least once a year, it also reviews each source of material and labor by inviting competitive bids from other vendors and trade contractors. Purchasing committees help create a healthy atmosphere in which cost control is a primary focus for everyone in the organization and for suppliers.

Job Cost Accounting

A good job cost accounting system is the ultimate management-by-exception tool. A detailed construction cost report is a key component of job cost accounting. It enables you to analyze actual costs and estimated cost variances and recognize problem areas in current or recent jobs so that you can control and prevent these problems in the future.

Job cost accounting lets you track material quality problems, trade contractor waste, and field supervision weaknesses. It's the next best thing to having a video camera on site to record jobsite activity. In the end, analyzing a detailed cost report takes far less time than watching 90 days' worth of videotape!

Construction Performance and Quality Control

Training field supervisors, employees, and trade contractors is also a large part of a successful cost control system. Issues such as materials handling, delivery policies, customer communications, and quality checkpoints all impact cost control.

Train at the Top

Superintendents and construction managers play a critical role in applying consistent quality inspections and demanding compliance with estimated specifications. A procedures manual that details company policies on all construction processes is your most valuable reference and training tool. Field supervisors are key players in your efforts to control costs during the construction process, so train them well. An ounce of instruction is worth a pound of problem solving.

Stick to Your Schedule

Construction schedules are the single most overlooked element of cost control. Carefully manage your schedule and you will be well on your way to managing costs.

Most builders will tell you it should take no more than 120 days to build a 2,000-square-foot home almost anywhere in the United States. Yet I have found that the average start-to-finish timetable is closer to 180 days. Guess what effect that 50% increase in cycle time has on profitability? The construction financing costs alone could wipe out the profit on many jobs.

Make sure all construction managers have their own copies of the construction schedule. You should continually reinforce the importance of sticking to the schedule.

Manage Quality to Manage Costs

Each construction manager and superintendent must have a copy of a quality control checklist that covers each major construction phase. A checklist makes it easier for superintendents to check for omissions, quality tolerances, and safety and cleanliness problems: All of these can add unnecessary costs. Mental lists are just not good enough. Your quality control checklist should be a written document that reminds supervisors to review the potential cost factor of each phase of construction. All too often, when replying on mental lists, even the most

veteran construction managers will forget to check a critical detail or two. Look at it this way: Airline pilots with 20 years of experience still use written checklists before every takeoff.

If you have several project supervisors, consider using a quality measurement tool to help senior managers identify problem areas that warrant better training and supervision.

Post-construction Review and System Improvement

Followup coupled with consistent team performance is the biggest obstacle most builders face when they set up cost-control systems. Too often, a builder designs a system and just hopes it will perform over time. However, constant efforts to refine business and construction systems are the keys to long-lasting cost control.

On a regular basis — perhaps after you complete each job — conduct a formal review of recent operations. This might involve one meeting, or several, focusing on what went right and what went wrong since the last review. Your goal is to identify areas of improvement and implement corrective action.

Benchmark your results against established goals so your team can measure success and help you figure out which areas need improvement. What kind of measures should you use? Monitor gross profit improvement, variance from budget levels, and individual cost components against established goals. Design a system to rate the cost-effectiveness of trade contractors, suppliers, and even types of materials. Review and summarize recent Q&C reports to spot trends. When you identify problems, seek cost-control ideas from everyone in your company. Be sure to give your team plenty of positive reinforcement when things are going well.

Hard Work Pays Off

Establishing and implementing a cost-control system is a time and labor-intensive process. It is also a process that must happen upfront. Your bank account won't swell within a month of implementing your system. But little by little, step by step, you can start to control your costs. And each small step moves you closer to your larger goal of business success.

Examining your company's operations under a microscope is hard work. But builders who pay close attention to the minute details of a successful construction cost control system can significantly boost their profitability. Big profits are built on small cost control measures. Content to superficially analyze costs, average builders also must be content with average profits. The difference is literally in the details.

Cost-Control Tips

Product Design & Engineering

- Base designs on the **standard dimensions** of structural products such as lumber and roof trusses.
- Don't routinely overbuild structural elements that buyers do not value. Offer them as **options** instead.
- Distribute **detailed plans** to all trades. Use them to explain cost-effective construction methods.

Construction Planning

- Before construction begins, speak with **everyone** involved in the home building process. Preconstruction conferences can help you identify potential problems before they start costing you money—and lost profits.

Bob Whitten is managing partner of SMA Consulting in Orlando, Fla. A former home builder, he is a frequent speaker at NAHB's International Builders' Show® and other industry conferences and symposiums. He can be reached at bwhitten@smaops.com.

Understanding Your Income Statement

Steven W. Hays Sr., CPA

An income statement is one of the most important tools for measuring a company's financial operating performance. This financial report summarizes revenues and expenses (in this case, costs of construction and operating expenses) and reflects the bottom line. The resulting net profit (or loss) is then included in the company's retained earnings or net worth.

This report ultimately measures a company's economic performance in "cost basis" numbers. Successful builders understand the importance of managing and monitoring their income statements.

Income Statement Elements

A "standard" home builder's income statement, as classified by NAHB's Chart of Accounts (available to NAHB members online at nahb.org/chart), consists of the following categories:

- **Sales:** all revenue generated from sales.

- **Developed lot costs:** the cost of the raw land and related development costs that result in a developed lot.

- **Direct construction costs:** known as "sticks and bricks," these are the major costs incurred in the construction of a new home. These costs can always be traced to a particular project and unit of construction.

- **Indirect construction costs:** other construction costs that cannot be easily and directly charged to a specific unit of construction.

- **Total costs of construction:** the sum of developed lot costs plus direct construction costs, plus indirect construction costs.

- **Gross profit:** sales minus the cost of goods sold (or construction).

- **Financial costs:** interest and other costs related to construction or development financing.

- **Selling expenses:** sales salaries and commissions, advertising, and model home expenses.

- **General and administrative expenses:** all "overhead" costs, including owner's compensation. Total operating expenses: the sum of financial costs, plus selling expenses, plus general and administrative expenses.

- **Net profit (loss) before income taxes:** literally the "bottom line" of an income statement.

Why Study an Income Statement?

Structuring an income statement according to NAHB's Chart of Accounts categories allows a home builders to better compare their company's financial performance against industry standards. When financial data is consistently classified into these categories, builders can compute meaningful financial ratios.

Financial ratios are important because they help builders understand how their company makes money, identify areas that require attention or different resources, and comprehend key financial ratios that are important to lenders (particularly debt-to-equity ratio and various returns on assets and sales).

For example, a builder can compute operating ratios by comparing the various costs and expenses on an income statement with the closed volume (sales) that also appears on the statement. The builder can then compare those operating ratios to industry operating ratios or to those of other builders.

Comparing operating ratios to industry ratios may inspire a builder to capitalize on favorable results, analyze future potential, or make changes based on unfavorable comparisons. Performing this type of financial analysis can help business owners improve their operating performance. Here are two important items to calculate and monitor:

- **Gross profit analysis.** The gross profit percentage (which consists of sales minus costs of construction) is a key financial measure. It represents a builder's ability to cover or absorb other operating expenses. If a builder cannot maintain an adequate gross profit margin, it's unlikely he or she can obtain an acceptable net profit. Maintaining an acceptable gross profit margin is essential to long-term economic viability.

- **Direct construction costs as a percentage of sales.** Managing this number is critical.

Direct construction costs are the largest cost a home builder incurs, yet some builders do very little to control these costs A common characteristic of successful builders is their ability to monitor and manage direct construction costs. Even a small reduction in direct construction costs as a percentage of the sales price can significantly increase a builder's bottom line. Any costs that can be removed or decreased from a house and multiplied with direct construction cost savings from other units can provide substantial income improvement.

At a minimum, income statements should be prepared and reviewed monthly and annually (the latter would show year-to-date figures). Results should be compared to similar periods from the prior year and to the current year's budget

The budget should be structured to display historical data in the same manner as the income statement in order to facilitate ease of comparing the documents, analyze the results, and making changes where necessary.

Understanding your income statement will make a significant difference in achieving higher profits and growth. Monitoring key ratios generated from the income statement will allow management to make better decisions. These ratios can help you determine, among other things, successful product lines and optimum staffing levels.

Steven Hays is Partner-in-Large of the Home Builders Services Group of RubinBrown LLP, Certified Public Accountants in St. Louis. RubinBrown provides accounting, tax, and business consulting services to more than 40 home building groups primarily in the Midwest. Reach Hays at 314-290-3336 or steve.hays@ rubinhrowncom.

Profitability Metrics: The Metrics of Home Building — The Starting Point!

Bob Whitten

My favorite aspect of my business life deals with what can be referred to as predictive behavior. Personality profiles and skills testing allow us to "predict" people's behavior and success at certain endeavors. Metrics work in the same way to predict and define the success of organizations and in some cases the individuals within those organizations.

My favorite books include *The Great Game of Business* and *Moneyball*; both have metrics of success (operational and financial statistics) at their very center. My favorite sport is baseball; greatly influenced by the ease of applying statistics or benchmarks of success to things like the relative value of an athlete and when to consider giving it up and retiring, etc.

I think you get the picture. I have spent the past 35 years learning how to apply operational and financial metrics to the home building industry to determine success, failure, when we are ready for expansion/contraction and how much we can afford to pay for everything from land to bookkeepers relative to your market conditions. I learn something new every week.

The Subsets of Metrics
• Budgeting and profitability
• Productivity
• Product and plan
• Cost control
• Marketing and market research
• Sales
• Customer

There are others potential metrics that are part of our business, but let's concentrate on the "accountability" metrics of home building. Those are the items that you can hold yourself and your team responsible for on a regular basis.

In some cases, we will be able to quote metric benchmarks for production and custom/semi-custom builders. In other cases, we will simply give you the formulas for the calculations where you can determine the benchmarks of success for your specific business model and market.

Budget and Profitability Metrics

These are the metrics of financial management, but they permeate every aspect of your home building business. Let's start with the Income Statement or Profit & Loss Statement benchmark metrics.

Income Statement Metric Goals by Builder Type

	NAHB COA	Production	Semi-Custom	Custom
Income	3100	100%	100%	100%
Less: COS	3600			
Land @ Market Value		17-22%	See note below	0%
Direct Construction Costs		52-57%	72%	77-79%
Gross Profit Margin		26%	28%	21-23%
Less: Operating Expenses	4000-8999			
Indirect Construction	4000-4999	4.0%	4.5%	5.0%
Finance	5000-5999	2.0%	1.0%	0%
Sales & Marketing	6000-6999	6.0-7.0%	5.0-6.0%	3.0-4.0%
General & Administrative (G&A)	8000-8999	4.0-5.0%	5.0-6.0%	4.0-5.0%
Total Expense		16.0-18.0%	15.5%-17.5%	12.0-14.0%
Net Profit From Homebuilding Operations		8.0-10.0%	10.5-12.5%	9.0-11.0%

Net Profit from Home building Operations = this is a pre-tax, pre-entrepreneurial expenses and pre- "OTHER" income calculation and represents the net profit calculation we should use for comparison between companies.

Types of "Other" Income for below the LINE = lot/land profit/loss, remodeling income, forfeited deposits, rental income/expense, interest income, etc.

The numbers can vary significantly whether you are a production builder, a semi-custom builder or custom builder. All of the percentages are based on total sales revenue from home building operations. This would exclude lot sales, remodeling work and rental income.

Let's start with a definition of

Production Builder = Builds exclusively from their own portfolio of plans on lots they own. Does build speculatively 10-90% of the time. Finances or uses their own capital to build every homes. Has a HUD closing for every home sold. May build multifamily for sale, as well as single-family.

Semi-Custom Builder = Builds from a portfolio of home plans but will consider/build a custom periodically. Will customize plans as they build on the lot/land of their customer as well as on their own lots. They may even build

a smaller percentage of their homes on spec (Perhaps 10-25% of total). We cannot quote a benchmark metric for land costs for a semi-custom builder as they may build some homes with and some without land. We combine their homes with land into the total cost of sales (COS) in the table above. Some of their homes will be self-financed and others will be done on the land and construction loan of the customer.

Custom Builder = The custom builder builds only one-of-a-kind homes. They build exclusively on the land of their customer. The customer finances the construction process 100%. This can be a design build firm or a construction only firm.

These benchmark metrics represent the average results of the top 20% of the home builders that have been measured over the past two (2014-2015) years of SMA Inner Circle membership (all SMA Clients included) and the past two

Indirect Construction Expense Subcategory Benchmark Metrics				
	NAHB COA	Production	Semi-Custom	Custom
Field & Supervision Expenses	4000-4499	2.0%	2.25-2.5%	2.75%
Warranty Expenses	4700-4799	.75%	.75%	.75%
Production Support Expenses	4800-4899	1.0%	1.25-1.5%	1.5%
Subdivision Maintenance Expense	4900-4999	.25%	0%	0%
Total Indirect Budget Metrics		**4.0%**	**4.5%**	**5.0%**

Subdivision Maintenance = Production builders often have to maintain street cleanliness and pay HOA dues upon taking down lots in a community.

Production Support Expenses = Purchasing, estimating and drafting salaries and expenses. Very large builders may also have a centralized scheduling department.

Warranty Expenses = Warranty salaries, trade costs for doing warranty work (often for other trades who are no longer employed by the builder) and costs of materials used during the warranty period of the homes.

Field & Supervision Expenses = Supervision payroll, punch-out labor and the payroll expenses of the direct managers of the construction supervisors go into this category. Also, truck expenses (including small tools and truck supplies) for the field team and their managers and cell phone and computer software and hardware used for field operations.

Sales & Marketing Expense Subcategory Benchmark Metrics				
	NAHB COA	Production	Semi-Custom	Custom
Commissions & Salaries	6000-6299	3.0-4.0%	2.5-3.5%	1.5-2.5%
Advertising	6300-6399	1.0%	1.0%	.75%
Model Home Expenses	6600-6699	.75%	1.0%	.50%
Other Sales & Marketing	6700-6799	1.25%	.5%	.25%
Total Sales & Marketing Budget Metrics		**6.0-7.0%**	**5.0-6.0%**	**3.0-4.0%**

Other Sales & Marketing = Market research, sales concessions (including paying buyer closing costs) and marketing salaries if position is exclusively marketing and buyer closing gifts.

Model Home Expenses = Costs to operate a model (including amortization of furniture and decor), costs to operate a design or selection center.

Advertising Expenses = Website amortization and maintenance, internet ads, print advertising, marketing signage of all types, billboards, truck signs/wraps and promotional events (home shows, parade of homes fees & expenses) etc.

Commissions & Salaries = Both in-house and co-broker commissions, sales, wages and bonuses paid to sales team including direct sales management and sales support.

2014 and 2016 NAHB *The Cost of Doing Business Studies.* These results are obviously skewed by the fact that only home builders of a certain level of business sophistication would participate in these studies or be clients of SMA.

In the above illustration, gross profit margin (GPM)is the key illustrated benchmark. Gross profit is the hardest to control and predict. When you master GPM to a consistent range and total, you have accomplished one of the most difficult tasks in business. Controlling overhead is easy in comparison and thus net profit becomes a simple by-product of the key GPM metric both in budgeting into the future and in actual results.

We want to encourage builders to be the best they can, not settle for the industry average.

Let's look in detail to two sections of the home builder operating expenses. We like to divide the indirect construction expenses into 3-4 subcategories and the sales and marketing into four subcategories for benchmarking purposes.

What is an entrepreneurial expense? The wife's BMW, the plane, the hunting lodge, the season tickets, etc.

Advertising Expenses = website amortization and maintenance, online and print advertising, marketing signage, billboards, truck signs/wraps and promotional events (home shows, parade of homes fees and expenses) etc.

Commissions and Salaries = both in-house and co broker commissions, sales, wages and bonus' paid to sales team including direct sales management and sales support.

Bob Whitten is managing partner of SMA Consulting in Orlando, Fla. A former home builder, he is a frequent speaker at NAHB's International Builders' Show and other industry conferences and symposiums. He can be reached at bwhitten@smaops.com.

2018 Cost of Doing Business Survey

I. FIRM'S PROFILE

1. Indicate your firm's main operation during fiscal year 2017 and write in the percentage of your business that operation represents.

	Main operation (Check ONE only)	Percent of Your Business
Single-family production builder	☐	_____ %
Single-family custom builder (on owner's lot)	☐	_____ %
Single-family custom builder (on builder's lot)	☐	_____ %
Multifamily builder (condo/co-op units)	☐	_____ %
Multifamily builder (for-rent units)	☐	_____ %
Land developer	☐	_____ %
Residential remodeling/rehabilitation	☐	_____ %
Other (specify)	☐	_____ %
	Total:	**100%**

2. How many years has your firm been in the residential construction business? _____ year(s)

3. Of the total number of single family-units your firm closed in fiscal year 2017, how many were pre-sold, speculative, and/or built on others' land (owners' lots)? *(If none in a category, please write zero.)*

	Single-Family Units Closed
Pre-sold (on builder's lot)	_____
Speculative	_____
Built on others' land (owners' lots)	_____
TOTAL	_____

II. FINANCIAL INFORMATION

4. Balance Sheet for fiscal year 2017.

Each code number refers to the NAHB Chart of Accounts, found at www.nahb.org/chart]			
Assets		**Liabilities and Owner's Equity**	
Cash [1000-1090]	$	Current Liabilities [2000-2490]	$
Receivables and Inventories [1200-1390]	$	Construction Loans Payable [2230]	$
Construction Work in Progress [1400-1490]	$	Long-term Loans Payable [2510, 2530]	$
Other Current Assets [1500-1690]	$	Other Long-Term Liabilities [2600-2890]	
Other Assets [1700-1990]	$	Owner's Equity [2900-2990]	$
Total Assets	$	Total Liabilities and Owner's Equity	$

Note: Total assets must equal the total of liabilities plus owner's equity.

5. Income Statement for fiscal year 2017.

*Each code number refers to the NAHB Chart of Accounts, found at www.nahb.org/chart		
Revenue from Operations		
Single-family Home Building [3100-3125]	$	
Residential Remodeling Revenue [3130]	$	
Multifamily Revenue [3140]	$	
Light Commercial/Industrial Revenue [3150]	$	
All Other Revenue [3000, 3050, 3160-3490]	$	
Total Company Revenue [sum of the previous five entries]		$
Cost of Sales		
Land Costs [3550]	$	
Single-family Home Building Direct Construction Costs [3600, 3610, 3620,3625] (permits, labor with burden, trade contractors, material costs, other unit-specific construction cost)	$	
Residential Remodeling Direct Construction Cost [3800-3899]	$	
Multifamily Direct Construction Costs [3640]	$	
Light Commercial/Industrial Direct Construction Costs [3650]	$	
Indirect Construction Costs [4000-4990] (job site and non-unit specific construction costs; include job supervision, estimating, purchasing and design personnel, warranty costs, construction vehicles, tools, and any other indirect costs)	$	
All Other Cost of Goods Sold (cost of sales related to items that fall under "All Other Revenue")	$	
Total Company Cost of Sales [sum of previous seven entries]		$
Gross Profit		
Total Company Revenue less Total Company Cost of Sales		$
Operating Expenses		
Financing Expenses [5000-5990] (points and interest on all loans)	$	
Sales and Marketing Expenses [6000-6990] (commissions, sales salaries and burden, advertising and sales promotion, and model home maintenance)	$	
General and Administrative Expenses [8000-8790; 8900-8990] (salaries, payroll taxes, and benefits of non job-related personnel; office & computer expenses, vehicles, travel, entertainment, taxes, insurance, professional services) (exclude owner's compensation)	$	
Depreciation [8800-8890]	$	
Owner's Compensation [8010] (owner's salary, draws, bonuses and benefits)	$	
Total Operating Expenses [sum of previous five entries]		$
Net Income Before Taxes [total company gross profit minus total operating expenses]		$

APPENDIX

V

Detailed Tables

Appendix V

V.1. Cost of Doing Business Study detailed tables

Q1. Indicate your Firm's Main Operation During Fiscal year 2017
(Percent of Respondents)

	Total	Region			Total 2017 Revenue ($ millions)			Number of Homes Closed				Type of Builder		
		Midwest	South	West	<2	2-9.9	≥10	<10	10-25	26-99	≥100	With land costs	Without land costs	Combination
Single-family production builder	38	32	36	52	33	29	68	12	33	67	64	63	6	33
Single-family custom builder (on owner's lot)	30	27	30	24	50	59	21	48	29	11	18	6	82	47
Single-family custom builder (on builder's lot)	18	23	23	5	8	12	11	17	24	22	18	31	12	20
Multifamily builder (condo/co-op units)	1	5							5					
Multifamily builder (for-rent units)	1							5	5					
Land Developer	2		4											
Residential remodeling/ rehabilitation	7	14	5	5				14						
Other	4	10	2	14	8			5	5					

Q1b. Percent of your business from each operation
(Average Share)

	Total	Region			Total 2017 Revenue ($ millions)			Number of Homes Closed				Type of Builder		
		Midwest	South	West	<2	2-9.9	≥10	<10	10-25	26-99	≥100	With land costs	Without land costs	Combination
Single-family production builder	32	31	31	37	34	28	55	12	32	46	58	56	4	25
Single-family custom builder - on owners lot	27	25	28	26	35	49	27	40	24	22	17	5	75	42
Single-family custom builder - on builders lot	17	18	21	8	11	9	10	15	22	20	15	29	6	20
Multifamily builder - condo/co-op units	1	3	0	3	0	0	3	0	4	3	1	1	0	1
Multifamily builder - for-rent units	1	0	1	0	0	0	1	0	2	1	2	0	0	1
Land Developer	2	0	3	2	2	1	1	3	1	4	1	2	0	2
Residential remodeling/rehabilitation	8	14	7	7	4	9	0	16	3	0	1	2	7	3
Other	11	10	9	17	15	3	3	13	11	5	6	5	7	6

V.1. Cost of Doing Business Study detailed tables (continued)

Q2. Years Firm Has Been in Residential Construction Business
(Percent of Respondents)

	Total	Region			Total 2017 Revenue ($ millions)			Number of Homes Closed				Type of Builder		
		Midwest	South	West	<2	2-9.9	≥10	<10	10-25	26-99	≥100	With land costs	Without land costs	Combination
Under 5 years	5		6	6	27	5	5	6		6	8	3	6	6
5-10 years	18	11	23	12	9	24	16	19	17	22	8	13	29	16
11-19 years	21	17	26	18	18	18	37	22	22	22	23	19	12	31
20-29 years	25	44	17	35	9	29	16	31	17	33	8	28	24	22
30+ Years	31	28	28	29	36	24	26	22	44	17	54	38	29	25
Average (Years)	23	31	20	23	22	23	25	20	29	20	32	29	19	21
Median (Years)	20	23	17	24	14	22	16	20	28	19	30	24	20	19

Q3. Of single-family units closed in 2017, indicate how many were pre-sold, speculative, and/or built on other's (owner's) land
(Average number of homes closed)

	Total	Region			Total 2017 Revenue ($ millions)			Number of Homes Closed				Type of Builder		
		Midwest	South	West	<2	2-9.9	≥10	<10	10-25	26-99	≥100	With land costs	Without land costs	Combination
Pre-Sold -on Builders lot	16	13	12	24	5	5	43	1	5	19	66	25	0	16
Speculative	12	10	12	10	6	3	31	1	6	16	40	14	0	15
Built on other's land -owner's lots	10	13	10	4	2	9	19	3	4	15	29	0	21	14
Total	38	36	34	38	13	17	93	4	15	49	135	39	21	45

V.I. Cost of Doing Business Study detailed tables *(continued)*

Q4. Balance Sheet
(Average in $1,000s)

	Total	Region			Total 2017 Revenue ($ millions)			Number of Homes Closed				Type of Builder		
		Midwest	South	West	<2	2-9.9	≥10	<10	10-25	26-99	≥100	With land costs	Without land costs	Combination
ASSETS														
Cash	626	359	709	742	182	242	1,265	202	266	739	1,109	686	307	469
Receivables and Inventories	588	369	461	980	413	437	901	302	525	1,138	672	674	441	583
Construction Work in Progress	5,155	5,973	4,662	4,424	244	1,316	11,901	415	1,208	5,181	15,699	5,282	432	6,279
Other Current Assets	907	845	971	858	166	84	2,169	106	112	978	1,089	636	48	589
Other Assets	758	747	485	1,183	141	740	1,237	138	1,574	800	1,502	1,350	125	608
Total Assets	8,034	8,292	7,288	8,186	1,146	2,818	17,474	1,163	3,685	8,836	20,071	8,628	1,353	8,528
LIABILITIES														
Current Liabilities	1,869	3,979	1,103	624	220	658	4,087	239	849	2,943	4,694	1,042	559	3,050
Construction Loans Payable	2,611	1,286	2,520	3,531	370	188	6,300	242	168	2,791	7,491	3,393	71	2,414
Long-term Loans Payable	749	780	961	360	173	449	1,461	104	26	985	1,624	1,010	23	526
Other Long-Term Liabilities	58	0	11	211	81	73	42	46	145	81	5	108	15	40
Owner's Equity	2,747	2,247	2,694	3,461	302	1,450	5,585	532	2,497	2,035	6,256	3,075	685	2,497
Total Liabilities and Owner's Equity	8,034	8,292	7,288	8,186	1,146	2,818	17,474	1,163	3,685	8,836	20,071	8,628	1,353	8,528

V.1. Cost of Doing Business Study detailed tables *(continued)*

Q5. Income Statement
(Average in $1,000s)

	Total	Region			Total 2017 Revenue			Number of Homes Closed				Type of Builder		
		Midwest	South	West	<2	2-9.9	≥10	<10	10-25	26-99	≥100	With land costs	Without land costs	Combination
Revenue														
Single-Family home building	15,686	17,582	13,046	17,658	1,099	5,009	33,683	2,431	7,998	17,716	37,977	13,801	5,750	19,083
Residential Remodeling	167	299	163	50	88	300	93	280	280	10	19	141	187	190
Multifamily home building	314	0	15	1,440	0	0	776	0	0	1,638	0	614	35	186
Light Commercial/Industrial	67	21	6	0	8	19	143	22	0	0	273	14	9	155
All Other Revenue	196	182	195	228	25	23	452	22	28	264	621	157	96	303
Total Company Revenue	16,429	18,084	13,425	19,377	1,221	5,350	35,147	2,755	8,305	19,628	38,890	14,726	6,076	19,917
Cost of Sales														
Land Costs	2,068	795	2,094	2,888	90	576	4,548	91	956	1,024	6,432	2,547	0	2,060
Single-family home building Direct Construction Costs	10,306	13,239	8,339	10,668	811	3,432	21,953	1,939	5,429	13,128	23,550	8,103	4,787	13,344
Residential Remodeling Direct Construction Costs	123	258	112	11	31	252	62	208	205	9	12	109	148	131
Multifamily Direct Construction Costs	249	0	13	1,142	0	0	617	0	0	1,302	0	509	30	126
Light Commercial/Industrial Direct Construction Costs	53	17	2	0	5	12	117	14	0	0	222	11	6	123
Indirect Construction Costs	469	542	392	429	71	156	979	80	213	443	1,189	363	103	641
All other Cost of Goods Sold	42	28	35	82	13	2	95	9	0	169	28	10	72	59
Total Company Cost of Sales	13,309	14,879	10,988	15,220	1,021	4,429	28,369	2,340	6,803	16,075	31,433	11,652	5,145	16,483
Gross Profit	3,120	3,205	2,438	4,157	200	921	6,778	415	1,502	3,553	7,457	3,074	931	3,434
Operating Expenses														
Financing Expenses	220	82	189	333	19	40	498	16	63	147	623	233	7	228
Sales and Marketing Expenses	779	915	684	651	44	192	1,730	27	289	537	2,327	670	38	1,027
General and Administrative Expenses	666	802	484	810	69	225	1,406	151	413	1,013	1,407	493	426	901
Depreciation	19	26	12	21	4	6	39	5	6	25	44	11	11	28
Owner's Compensation	194	173	204	205	33	140	337	96	168	244	264	153	191	186
Total Operating Expenses	1,879	1,997	1,573	2,020	169	602	4,011	295	939	1,966	4,664	1,559	673	2,370
Net Income Before Taxes	1,241	1,208	864	2,137	32	318	2,767	120	564	1,587	2,792	1,514	258	1,064

V.1. Cost of Doing Business Study detailed tables *(continued)*

Q5. Income Statement
(% Share of Revenue)

	Total	Region			Total 2017 Revenue			Number of Homes Closed				Type of Builder		
		Midwest	South	West	<2	2-9.9	≥10	<10	10-25	26-99	≥100	With land costs	Without land costs	Combination
Revenue														
Single-Family home building	95.5	97.2	97.2	91.1	90.1	93.6	95.8	88.2	96.3	90.3	97.7	93.7	94.6	95.8
Residential Remodeling	1.0	1.7	1.2	0.3	7.2	5.6	0.3	10.2	3.4	0.0	0.0	1.0	3.1	1.0
Multifamily home building	1.9	0.0	0.1	7.4	0.0	0.0	2.2	0.0	0.0	8.3	0.0	4.2	0.6	0.9
Light Commercial/Industrial	0.4	0.1	0.0	0.0	0.7	0.3	0.4	0.8	0.0	0.0	0.7	0.1	0.2	0.8
All Other Revenue	1.2	1.0	1.5	1.2	2.0	0.4	1.3	0.8	0.3	1.3	1.6	1.1	1.6	1.5
Total Company Revenue	100.0	100.0	100.0	100.0	100.0	100.0	100.0	100.0	100.0	100.0	100.0	100.0	100.0	100.0
Cost of Sales														
Land Costs	12.6	4.4	15.6	14.9	7.4	10.8	12.9	3.3	11.5	5.2	16.5	17.3	0.0	10.3
Single-family home building Direct Construction Costs	62.7	73.2	62.1	55.1	66.4	64.1	62.5	70.4	65.4	66.9	60.6	55.0	78.8	67.0
Residential Remodeling Direct Construction Costs	0.8	1.4	0.8	0.1	2.5	4.7	0.2	7.5	2.5	0.0	0.0	0.7	2.4	0.7
Multifamily Direct Construction Costs	1.5	0.0	0.1	5.9	0.0	0.0	1.8	0.0	0.0	6.6	0.0	3.5	0.5	0.6
Light Commercial/Industrial Direct Construction Costs	0.3	0.1	0.0	0.0	0.4	0.2	0.3	0.5	0.0	0.0	0.6	0.1	0.1	0.6
Indirect Construction Costs	2.9	3.0	2.9	2.2	5.8	2.9	2.8	2.9	2.6	2.3	3.1	2.5	1.7	3.2
All other Cost of Goods Sold	0.3	0.2	0.3	0.4	1.0	0.0	0.3	0.3	0.0	0.9	0.1	0.1	1.2	0.3
Total Company Cost of Sales	81.0	82.3	81.8	78.5	83.6	82.8	80.7	84.9	81.9	81.9	80.8	79.1	84.7	82.8
Gross Profit	19.0	17.7	18.2	21.5	16.4	17.2	19.3	15.1	18.1	18.1	19.2	20.9	15.3	17.2
Operating Expenses														
Financing Expenses	1.3	0.5	1.4	1.7	1.5	0.8	1.4	0.6	0.8	0.7	1.6	1.6	0.1	1.1
Sales and Marketing Expenses	4.7	5.1	5.1	3.4	3.6	3.6	4.9	1.0	3.5	2.7	6.0	4.5	0.6	5.2
General and Administrative Expenses	4.1	4.4	3.6	4.2	5.7	4.2	4.0	5.5	5.0	5.2	3.6	3.4	7.0	4.5
Depreciation	0.1	0.1	0.1	0.1	0.3	0.1	0.1	0.2	0.1	0.1	0.1	0.1	0.2	0.1
Owner's Compensation	1.2	1.0	1.5	1.1	2.7	2.6	1.0	3.5	2.0	1.2	0.7	1.0	3.1	0.9
Total Operating Expenses	11.4	11.0	11.7	10.4	13.8	11.3	11.4	10.7	11.3	10.0	12.0	10.6	11.1	11.9
Net Income Before Taxes	7.6	6.7	6.4	11.0	2.6	5.9	7.9	4.3	6.8	8.1	7.2	10.3	4.3	5.3

V.2. All single-family builders

Top 25% and bottom 25% by net profit margin
Income statement
(average in $1,000s)

	ALL	Top 25%	Bottom 25%
Revenue			
Single-Family home building	15,686	27,966	7,241
Residential Remodeling	167	294	158
Multifamily	314	1,004	0
Light Commercial/Industrial	67	0	3
All Other Revenue	196	267	263
Total Revenue	16,429	29,531	7,665
Costs of Sales			
Land Costs	2,068	4,672	1,387
Single-family home building Direct Construction Costs	10,306	16,439	4,844
Residential Remodeling Direct Construction Costs	123	213	91
Multifamily Direct Construction Costs	249	832	0
Light Commercial/Industrial Direct Construction Costs	53	0	2
Indirect Construction Costs	469	825	262
All other Costs of Goods Sold	42	19	13
Total Cost of Sales	13,309	23,000	6,599
Gross Profit	**3,120**	**6,531**	**1,066**
Operating Expenses			
Financing Expense	220	526	77
Sales and Marketing Expense	779	1,405	310
General and Administrative Expense	666	886	484
Depreciation	19	31	9
Owner's Compensation	194	319	104
Total Operating Expenses	1,879	3,168	984
Net Income Before Taxes	**1,241**	**3,363**	**82**

V.2. All single-family builders

Top 25% and bottom 25% by net profit margin
Income statement
(% share of revenue)

	ALL	Top 25%	Bottom 25%
Revenue			
Single-Family home building	95.5	94.7	94.5
Residential Remodeling	1.0	1.0	2.1
Multifamily	1.9	3.4	0.0
Light Commercial/Industrial	0.4	0.0	0.0
All Other Revenue	1.2	0.9	3.4
Total Revenue	100.0	100.0	100.0
Costs of Sales			
Land Costs	12.6	15.8	18.1
Single-faily home building Direct Construction Costs	62.7	55.7	63.2
Residential Remodeling Direct Construction Costs	0.8	0.7	1.2
Multifamily Direct Construction Costs	1.5	2.8	0.0
Light Commercial/Industrial Direct Construction Costs	0.3	0.0	0.0
Indirect Construction Costs	2.9	2.8	3.4
All other Costs of Goods Sold	0.3	0.1	0.2
Total Cost of Sales	81.0	77.9	86.1
Gross Profit	**19.0**	**22.1**	**13.9**
Operating Expenses			
Financing Expense	1.3	1.8	1.0
Sales and Marketing Expense	4.7	4.8	4.1
General and Administrative Expense	4.1	3.0	6.3
Owner's Compensation	1.2	1.1	1.4
Total Operating Expenses	11.4	10.7	12.8
Net Income Before Taxes	**7.6**	**11.4**	**1.1**

Balance sheet
(average in $1,000s)

	ALL	Top 25%	Bottom 25%
ASSETS			
Cash	626	1,474	314
Receivables and Inventories	588	447	875
Construction Work in Progress	5,155	9,325	3,822
Other Current assets	907	2,709	190
Other Assets	758	2,019	430
Total Assets	8,034	15,974	5,631
LIABILITIES			
Current Liabilities	1,869	1,512	755
Construction Loans Payable	2,611	6,068	1,517
Long-Term Loans Payable	749	1,679	917
Other Long-Term Liabilities	58	101	81
Owner's Equity	2,747	6,615	2,361
Total Liabilities and Owner's Equity	8,034	15,974	5,631

V.3. All single-family builders

Small-volume vs. production builders*

Income statement
(average in $1,000s)

	ALL	Small-Volume	Production
Revenue			
Single-Family home building	15,686	4,081	28,380
Residential Remodeling	167	280	14
Multifamily	314	0	776
Light Commercial/Industrial	67	15	143
All Other Revenue	196	24	452
Total Revenue	16,429	4,400	29,766
Costs of Sales			
Land Costs	2,068	347	3,870
Single-family home building Direct Construction Costs	10,306	2,973	18,613
Residential Remodeling Direct Construction Costs	123	207	11
Multifamily Direct Construction Costs	249	0	617
Light Commercial/Industrial Direct Construction Costs	53	10	117
Indirect Construction Costs	469	119	836
All other Costs of Goods Sold	42	6	95
Total Cost of Sales	13,309	3,662	24,158
Gross Profit	**3,120**	**737**	**5,608**
Operating Expenses			
Financing Expense	220	30	398
Sales and Marketing Expense	779	104	1,479
General and Administrative Expense	666	229	1,220
Depreciation	19	5	35
Owner's Compensation	194	118	254
Total Operating Expenses	1,879	486	3,386
Net Income Before Taxes	**1,241**	**251**	**2,221**

Small-volume builders closed on 25 or fewer homes in 2017. Production builders closed on 26 or more homes.

V.3. All single-family builders

Small-volume vs. production builders*
Income statement
(% share of revenue)

	ALL	Small-Volume	Production
Revenue			
Single-Family home building	95.5	92.7	95.3
Residential Remodeling	1.0	6.4	0.0
Multifamily	1.9	0.0	2.6
Light Commercial/Industrial	0.4	0.3	0.5
All Other Revenue	1.2	0.5	1.5
Total Revenue	100.0	100.0	100.0
Costs of Sales			
Land Costs	12.6	7.9	13.0
Single-faily home building Direct Construction Costs	62.7	67.6	62.5
Residential Remodeling Direct Construction Costs	0.8	4.7	0.0
Multifamily Direct Construction Costs	1.5	0.0	2.1
Light Commercial/Industrial Direct Construction Costs	0.3	0.2	0.4
Indirect Construction Costs	2.9	2.7	2.8
All other Costs of Goods Sold	0.3	0.1	0.3
Total Cost of Sales	81.0	83.2	81.2
Gross Profit	**19.0**	**16.8**	**18.8**
Operating Expenses			
Financing Expense	1.3	0.7	1.3
Sales and Marketing Expense	4.7	2.4	5.0
General and Administrative Expense	4.1	5.2	4.1
Depreciation	0.1	0.1	0.1
Owner's Compensation	1.2	2.7	0.9
Total Operating Expenses	11.4	11.0	11.4
Net Income Before Taxes	**7.6**	**5.7**	**7.5**

Balance sheet
(average in $1,000s)

	ALL	Small-Volume	Production
ASSETS			
Cash	626	218	924
Receivables and Inventories	588	358	905
Construction Work in Progress	5,155	613	10,440
Other Current assets	907	107	1,034
Other Assets	758	497	1,151
Total Assets	8,034	1,794	14,454
LIABILITIES			
Current Liabilities	1,869	392	3,819
Construction Loans Payable	2,611	224	5,141
Long-Term Loans Payable	749	84	1,305
Other Long-Term Liabilities	58	71	43
Owner's Equity	2,747	1,024	4,146
Total Liabilities and Owner's Equity	8,034	1,794	14,454

V.4. Single-family builders with land costs

Small-volume vs. production builders*

Income statement
(average in $1,000s)

	ALL	Small-Volume
Revenue		
Single-Family home building	13,801	3,725
Residential Remodeling	141	236
Multifamily	614	0
Light Commercial/Industrial	14	25
All Other Revenue	157	11
Total Revenue	14,726	3,997
Costs of Sales		
Land Costs	2,547	788
Single-family home building Direct Construction Costs	8,103	2,076
Residential Remodeling Direct Construction Costs	109	184
Multifamily Direct Construction Costs	509	0
Light Commercial/Industrial Direct Construction Costs	11	20
Indirect Construction Costs	363	99
All other Costs of Goods Sold	10	0
Total Cost of Sales	11,652	3,167
Gross Profit	**3,074**	**830**
Operating Expenses		
Financing Expense	233	64
Sales and Marketing Expense	670	175
General and Administrative Expense	493	165
Depreciation	11	2
Owner's Compensation	153	93
Total Operating Expenses	1,559	500
Net Income Before Taxes	**1,514**	**330**

* Small-volume builders closed on 25 or fewer homes in 2017. Production builders closed on 26 or more homes.

V.4. Single-family builders with land costs

Small-volume vs. production builders*
Income statement
(% share of revenue)

	ALL	Small-Volume
Revenue		
Single-Family home building	93.7	93.2
Residential Remodeling	1.0	5.9
Multifamily	4.2	0.0
Light Commercial/Industrial	0.1	0.6
All Other Revenue	1.1	0.3
Total Revenue	100.0	100.0
Costs of Sales		
Land Costs	17.3	19.7
Single-faily home building Direct Construction Costs	55.0	51.9
Residential Remodeling Direct Construction Costs	0.7	4.6
Multifamily Direct Construction Costs	3.5	0.0
Light Commercial/Industrial Direct Construction Costs	0.1	0.5
Indirect Construction Costs	2.5	2.5
All other Costs of Goods Sold	0.1	0.0
Total Cost of Sales	79.1	79.2
Gross Profit	**20.9**	**20.8**
Operating Expenses		
Financing Expense	1.6	1.6
Sales and Marketing Expense	4.5	4.4
General and Administrative Expense	3.4	4.1
Depreciation	0.1	0.1
Owner's Compensation	1.0	2.3
Total Operating Expenses	10.6	12.5
Net Income Before Taxes	**10.3**	**8.3**

V.5. Combination single-family builders

Small-volume vs. production builders*

Balance sheet

(average in $1,000s)

	ALL	Small-Volume	Production
ASSETS			
Cash	469	264	694
Receivables and Inventories	583	126	1,086
Construction Work in Progress	6,279	515	12,618
Other Current Assets	589	105	1,122
Other Assets	608	106	1,160
Total Assets	8,528	1,116	16,681
LIABILITIES			
Current Liabilities	3,050	363	6,006
Construction Loans Payable	2,414	148	4,907
Long-term Loans Payable	526	22	1,081
Other Long-Term Liabilities	40	7	77
Owner's Equity	2,497	576	4,610
Total Liabilities and Owner's Equity	8,528	1,116	16,681

Small-volume builders closed on 25 or fewer homes in 2017. Production builders closed on 26 or more homes.

Glossary

accounts payable. The amount of money a business owes for products and services purchased on credit.

accounts receivable. The amount of money owed to a business for products and services provided on credit.

assets. Property or items of tangible or intangible value such as accounts receivable, prepaid expenses, and organization costs that a business owns.

balance sheet. A report of the financial condition of an institution that lists the assets, liabilities, and owner's equity at a particular date; sometimes called a "statement of financial position."

builders with land costs. Builders who build only on their own lots.

builders without land costs. Builders who build exclusively on their customers' land.

capital. Money or assets supplied by banks, investors, or owners of a business. The dollar value of assets contributed to a business.

chart of accounts. A list of all accounts, and their assigned account numbers, used in recording financial transactions.

combination builders. Builders who build both speculative/presold homes on their own land and custom homes on their customers' land.

current assets. Assets that could be used up or converted to cash within the next operating cycle of the business, usually one year.

current liabilities. Debts that must be paid within the next operating cycle of a business, usually one year.

current ratio. A liquidity measure that indicates a company's ability to meet its current liabilities. The relationship between current assets and current liabilities calculated by dividing the dollar amount of current assets by the dollar amount of current liabilities.

debt-to-equity ratio. A measure of leverage in a business equal to the amount of long-term debt divided by the amount of equity contributed by the owners.

expense. The necessary payments associated with a period of time that are used to operate a home building business. Expenses reduce revenue. *See also* financing expenses, general expenses, and sales and marketing expenses.

financing expenses. All interest, points, and service charges related to financing construction activities or company purchases; all closing costs, such as points, taxes, fees, and other miscellaneous charges.

financial ratios. Ratios that identify relationships between different classifications in the financial statements to more clearly define a company's financial strength, efficiency of operation, and return on investment.

general and administrative expenses. Expenses that cannot be classified in other expense categories, such as training and education, charitable contributions, and trade association dues.

gross profit on sales. Total revenue minus cost of goods it sold, excluding financing, selling, and administrative expenses.

income statement. A report on business operations showing net income or net loss for a fiscal period; sometimes called a "profit and loss statement."

liabilities. Amounts owed to creditors; the claims of creditors to the assets of the business.

liquidity. The capacity to turn assets into cash.

leverage. The degree to which a business uses borrowed money to finance its assets.

loans payable. Long-term liabilities representing obligations of the company which are due over a period of time. Examples include notes payable and mortgages.

net income. The amount of revenue that remains after deducting costs and expenses for a period.

net loss. The amount by which total costs and expenses exceed total revenue.

net sales. The invoice value of sales minus discounts, returns, or allowances.

operating expenses. The cost of transacting normal business operations, excluding cost of goods sold, interest, and taxes.

owner's compensation. The amount of money an owner would make doing similar work for another company as an employee.

owner's equity. Owner's claims to the assets of the business. Assets minus liabilities.

production builder. A home builder with 26 or more closings per year.

production combination builder. A home builder with 26 or more closings per year who builds both speculative/presold homes on his or her own land and custom homes on customers' land.

production builder with land costs. A home builder with 26 or more closings per year who builds only on his or her own lots

profit. The amount of revenue that remains after deducting costs and expenses for a period of time.

return on equity. Reward for the owners' capital investment.

revenue. Amount collected for goods and services provided; sales.

sales and marketing expenses. All expenses associated with selling homes, such as advertising expenses, inhouse and broker commissions, models, brochures, and signs.

schedule of accounts payable. A list of all creditors in the accounts payable ledger, the balance in each account, and the total amount owed to all creditors.

schedule of accounts receivable. A list of each charge customer, the balance in the customer's account, and the total amount due from all customers.

small-volume builder. A home builder with 25 or fewer closings per year.

small-volume builder with land costs. A small-volume builder who only builds spec or presold homes on lots the builder owns.

small-volume builder without land costs. A home builder with 25 or fewer closings per year who builds only on land the customer owns.

small-volume combination builder. A home builder with 25 or fewer closings per year who builds both speculative/presold homes on his or her own land and custom homes on customers' land.

working capital. Current assets of a business that can be applied to its current operations; current assets minus current liabilities.